About the Author

Carole Phillips was born in1947 in Sussex but brought up in post war Tyneside. These were hard times, but taught Carole to be resourceful, determined and laugh at adversity. Carole's police career was from 1966 – 2000 in various ranks from Special Constable to Superintendent. She now lives in Devon and is a guest speaker telling her policing stories with candour and humour.

I dedicate this book to police colleagues past and present, especially those who continue to face all the challenges of modern policing with courage and determination.

Carole Phillips

BLUE LINE- PINK THREAD

MEMOIRS OF POLICE OFFICER CAROLE PHILLIPS

AUSTIN MACAULEY
PUBLISHERS LTD.

A CIP catalogue record for this title is available from the British Library.

ISBN 9781786126412 (Paperback)
ISBN 9781786126429 (Hardback)
ISBN 9781786126436 (E-Book)

www.austinmacauley.com

First Published (2015)
Austin Macauley Publishers Ltd.
25 Canada Square
Canary Wharf
London
E14 5LQ

The photographs within this book have been credited wherever possible, with permission given from the named sources. The author has attempted to find the appropriate recognition for each photograph, however gaining contact was not always possible and therefore not every source could be provided.

Cover photograph courtesy of the Bedford Times & Citizen.

Acknowledgments

My heartfelt thanks to my husband Martin and daughter Michelle for their love and support throughout my career and in the writing of this book. None of it would have been possible without them.
I also want to thank my publishers Austin Macauley for their invaluable help with the completion and publication of this book.

Introduction

Carole joined the police service at a time when women were treated as separate threads of the organisation; specialising in dealing with women and children. Policewomen wore skirts and stockings, carried handbags and were regarded by many as the weaker sex, not to be utilised in frontline policing. Nonetheless, as long as they knew their place, rather like a sewing kit, they were handy to keep on one side, because they often proved very useful.

Policewomen of Carole's time knew no different, as the thin blue line had always been regarded as 'men's work'. Carole was happy working in the Policewomen's Department, but occasionally got an insight into general police duties and she liked what she saw. When the opportunity arose, she was keen to pioneer the changes, which led to integration and equality. She faced the many challenges with determination and a sense of humour, which gained her acceptance among her male colleagues.

Unlike many police memoirs, this is not a cynical story of a woman's struggles, but it is an amusing, enlightening and truly unique story that will enthral its readers and give them an insight into Carole's police career from 1966 – 2000. She eventually achieved the rank of Superintendent and says she witnessed how women officers were gradually woven into the fabric of the 'blue line'. In the early days women were used like threads to fill in gaps in the fabric, but eventually, after the Equal Pay Act and Sex Discrimination Act, they became an integral part of the service, making it stronger and more versatile.

2015 officially celebrates 100 years of Women Police. The pace of change has been relentless, especially in the last fifty years, so it is fitting that 'Blue Line – Pink Thread' now provides an entertaining historical account of social change in the police service and in British society during that period.

Chapter 1

Getting in Line

It always seems to me that life is a succession of roleplays; none of us are sure that we can do something until we step into role and give it our best. Suddenly, the things that seemed impossible become possible, others start to believe in us and so our confidence grows. That is how it was with me becoming a police officer.

In 1965 my name was Carole Mitchell and I was eighteen years old. I was working as a library assistant at Hemel Hempstead Library. It was whilst working there, that I often glanced out of the window at all the activity and excitement going on in the back yard of the Police Station next door. I was mesmerised as I watched uniformed officers literally run to their cars and speed off to incidents with blue lights flashing. Then, later they would return with prisoners and stride purposefully to the back door of the police station, with that slight arrogance of a job well done.

Meanwhile, I catalogued or shelved books, dealt with requests, went out on the mobile library or read stories to young children. I enjoyed my work, but it lacked excitement in comparison to the action next door,

During the summer months, when I had the office window open, I occasionally got into conversation with police officers as they went about their duties in the police station yard. It hadn't escaped my attention that many of them were young, fit, good-looking men, and as an eighteen year old I rather enjoyed their attention. They always seemed a happy, well-motivated group and I wondered what it would be like to be part of such a team. I eventually got the chance to find out more when I was invited to a social event taking place at the police station. It soon became apparent that, when off duty, police officers let their hair down, or at least ruffled their short tidy haircuts, to enjoy a good social life. Most police stations had a bar on the premises to facilitate section or divisional socials and Hemel Hempstead was no exception. I enjoyed the lively sense of humour and the camaraderie and after meeting a few policewomen was eventually persuaded to join the Special Constabulary.

Together with other volunteer Special Constables, I attended a course of local training at the police station. Each training session lasted a few hours every week, over the course of several months, providing us with sufficient knowledge to act in a support role. We were then provided with a uniform, sworn in before a magistrate and issued with a warrant card. Then it was time to let us loose on the unsuspecting public. 'Specials' were often referred to as 'Hobby Bobbies' by regular officers because, although we had full police powers, we were volunteers and less competent than our fully trained colleagues. There was also a feeling amongst some regular officers that our voluntary duty took away their opportunity for paid overtime.

Nonetheless, we were providing a useful visible presence on foot patrol, covering cinema or school crossing patrols, or in making up the numbers for special events such as carnivals. We had insignia with 'SC' on our lapels and cap badge, but members of the public usually didn't know the difference between a 'regular' and a 'special'.

I was feeling excited, but apprehensive, when I first stepped out as a Special Constable on the streets of Hemel Hempstead. Initially, I patrolled with a regular officer either on a 'foot beat' or in a car, but after a few weeks, I was given a town centre foot beat on my own. Sometimes, as I patrolled down the main shopping street, I would glance at my reflection in a shop window and feel very proud to be wearing a police uniform, which in those days seemed to command respect from the public. Policewomens' uniform was still very traditional with white shirts, tie, belted jacket, knee length skirt, stockings and black lace-up shoes. There were no personal radios, so I needed to use my initiative in dealing with any incident that arose. Quite often people would just stop for a chat or to ask directions. My local knowledge was quite good, but I carried a street map to fill in any gaps, because I didn't want to appear incompetent.

I tended to work for two or three hours on two evenings a week and also covered the Saturday morning crossing patrol outside the Odeon Cinema. A more experienced police officer taught me basic traffic control signals, handed me a pair of white gauntlet style gloves and then I was on my own. When the cinema doors opened and hundreds of excited children came rushing out to cross the road, it was essential to either be authoritarian or expect to be trampled in the rush. This was my first experience of roleplaying the part of a police officer and enjoying the authority given by wearing a police uniform. It always amazed me that although I was an inexperienced young driver and would command no respect on the road, when on crossing patrol duty as a young Special Constable, a clear hand signal was all that was required to bring busy traffic to a standstill.

One of the most memorable duties as a Special Constable was when Roger Moore, who played the Saint in the popular 1960s TV series, came to Hemel Hempstead for a special showing of the Saint at the Pavilion Theatre. I helped with security and was then invited to sit next to him in the theatre. He was very dashing and very charming. I don't think he said much to me, but I was impressed just to meet him, especially since he later took on the role of James Bond.

I enjoyed variety in my life, so when I wasn't on duty at the library or as a Special Constable, I worked evening shifts as a barmaid at the 'Leather Bottle' Pub in Leverstock Green, Hemel Hempstead. I felt that I had three distinct roles to play and different clothes and hairstyles to fit each role; the quiet, serious librarian, the smart, confident Special Constable and the efficient, friendly barmaid. I didn't have any particular life plan or career aspirations and was quite happy to seize opportunities when they presented themselves and earn enough money to cover my immediate needs. I was living with my parents and younger sister in the family home; a council house at Bennetts End, Hemel Hempstead, so I enjoyed all the benefits of family life. In 1968 my family moved to Biggleswade, Bedfordshire, where my father was to be manager of 'Doddimeads' furniture store and we would live in the flat above the shop. My finances and my options were limited, so I decided to go with them, which meant that I had to resign from Hertfordshire Special Constabulary. 'Doddimeads of Biggleswade' sounded like something from a TV comedy, but this was an unwanted upheaval for me, and not a particularly happy time in my life. My two older brothers had left home and joined the Royal Air Force and my younger sister quickly settled into her new home and school. I missed my job, my friends and the vibrant life of new town Hemel Hempstead.

I needed to make a fresh start and establish myself as part of the local community, so I decided to apply to join Bedfordshire Special Constabulary. I was accepted and attended the monthly training sessions at Greyfriars Police

Station in Bedford. This was my first experience of being part of a 'big family', realising that wherever a police officer goes, she will be part of a shared culture and have transferrable skills. My duties were mainly based at Biggleswade Police Station, from where I went on foot patrol around the town or on vehicle patrol with a regular officer. I particularly enjoyed foot patrol on Saturdays around the busy market, as I had a chance to get to know the stall-holders, shopkeepers and members of the public.

Occasionally, I would deal with a shoplifter or a minor assault, or be called in to the station to assist with a female prisoner, but most of my time was spent on easy-going public relations. Biggleswade tended to go to sleep early, so evening duty was less interesting and involved non-eventful foot patrol around the town or routine pub visits with a regular officer. Occasionally, I would assist at special events in Bedford and enjoyed being part of a big team and being delegated a specific task.

Being a Special Constable was challenging and good fun, but I also needed full-time employment. Although I lived with my parents, I needed to be able to pay my way, so I got a job as a wage clerk for the United Counties Bus Company in Bedford. The bus station and offices were directly opposite the police station in Greyfriars, so once again I was able to watch the police action on a day-to-day basis. It wasn't long before I realised that routine office work wasn't for me. I needed variety and excitement in my work, so I decided to make the commitment to become a full-time police officer. I knew that this would require hard work and dedication, but I was ready to accept the challenge. There was a freeze on recruitment in most Police Forces at that time, so I sent off applications to Bedfordshire & Luton Constabulary and the Metropolitan Police, intending to accept the first offer that came my way.

In February 1969 I was at home in Biggleswade, when the post arrived and I saw a large brown, official looking envelope, addressed to me. I felt a sudden wave of excitement, tore open the envelope and read the important words, 'I am pleased to inform you that you have been accepted as a Constable in Bedfordshire and Luton Constabulary. Appointment is conditional on successful completion of the National Police Training Course and a two-year period as a probationary constable. You are required to report to the Training Office at Police Headquarters, The Pines, Goldington Road, Bedford, at 9am on Monday 31st March 1969. Smart civilian clothing should be worn.' I read the letter twice just to make sure that I wasn't missing anything and then gave a "whoop" of delight. At last, I had made it. A new door was about to open and I could say goodbye to being a wage clerk. I didn't know quite what to expect at Police Training School, but felt sure that I would find it exciting and challenging. I hoped that my three years' experience as a Special Constable would stand me in good stead, although being a regular officer was undoubtedly a lot different to being an unpaid volunteer.

That evening I told my parents the good news and they were clearly delighted and no doubt relieved that I had finally settled on my chosen career. On leaving Apsley Grammar School at the age of eighteen, I had decided that university wasn't for me, especially as I knew that funding student life would have been difficult. My father was a furniture shop manager and my mother worked part-time in a dry-cleaning shop, so finances were limited. None of my family had ever gone to university, but we all had a strong work ethic, so I had been keen to start earning a wage. Careers advice at school was almost non-existent for girls who didn't want to go on to higher education or be secretaries, nurses or teachers. For several years, I had enjoyed a Saturday job at Hemel Hempstead Library, so I applied for a job as a full-time library assistant and was accepted. Although it wasn't exciting, I had soon settled down and found the work varied and interesting. I might have continued working at the library had it not have been for the family move, but now circumstances had taken me in a new direction.

On reflection, I realise that I had always liked uniforms and the sense of belonging to a disciplined, well organised team. I had been a Girl Guide, a Land Ranger and a Special Constable, so it was odds-on that I would choose a job in uniform. The police service now seemed to offer the right career choice and I was ready to take on the challenge.

Monday 31st March 1969 could not come quickly enough, and on that morning, dressed in my smartest civilian clothes, I reported to Police Headquarters (HQ). Although the main building, known as 'The Pines' was a fine Edwardian style manor house in Goldington Road, Bedford, the training department was situated in two Portakabins around the back of the building.

I was one of four new recruits who would undertake a local induction course, followed by a thirteen week Initial Police Training Course at a District Training Centre. The other three new recruits were men and we all seemed to be getting on well together, so I was disappointed when I learned that they would be attending a training course at Eynsham Hall, Oxfordshire, which was an all-male establishment. I would eventually be found a place at a Police Training Centre, which accepted female officers. This was to be the first of many occasions that I would be separated from my male colleagues and I soon realised that whereas they would bond together in shared experiences, I would have to be independent and hope to make friends along the way.

The formal induction course at Police HQ took place during our first week. We were allocated our police 'collar numbers', so-called as they used to be located on the high-necked tunics. They were now attached to epaulettes and would be better described as shoulder numbers, but old habits die hard in the police service. Induction included being issued with uniform and equipment. When I saw the store man I expected to hand in my Special Constabulary uniform and be given brand new uniform for training school, but I was mistaken. We were to have two full uniforms for training school and he decided that, with a few modifications, my already second-hand 'Specials' uniform would suffice. I was given new numbers for the epaulettes, and had to remove the 'Specials' shoulder flashes. The fact that this left holes and stitch marks in the material did not seem to concern the store-man, but I liked to take pride in my appearance and felt that it was sub-standard. The other uniform issued was to become my best uniform for drill and parades. Whereas, my male colleagues seemed to have a good range of sizes from which to choose, I found that female officers were required to 'fit' what was in stock and the choice was fairly limited. My skirt was too long and my jacket was too tight, but I was assured that the tailor would take things up and ease a few seams here and there. The storeman explained that, once I had made it through training school, I could have a uniform tailor made. The Force did not recruit enough women to justify having a wide selection of sizes and a new uniform would be a waste until I had proved myself. I did not find this terribly helpful or reassuring, but I didn't feel in any position to argue. The tailor made the adjustments and if I breathed in, I would be comfortable!

The uniform issue for a woman included six shirts with detachable starched collars. Perhaps women's necks are more delicate than those of their male colleagues, because I soon found out that, after eight hours of duty, the stiff ridge at the top of the collar left a red line around my neck and the collar stud left an uncomfortable imprint just below the Adam's apple. We were also issued with a black tie, two skirts, two tunics, a mackintosh, a great coat, a cape, hat, handbag and a box containing twelve pairs of black seamed stockings. Tights and trousers were not allowed, so suspender belts and stockings were standard. The uniform was impractical and I was under the impression that it must have been designed by a man!

We had to buy our own flat, black lace-up shoes and would receive a shoe allowance. Initially, I bought a pair of fairly soft leather shoes from a local store, but I soon realised that the leather, particularly that on the toe caps needed to be hard in order to hold a bright polished sheen.

There was a written uniform code for female officers, stating that makeup should be kept to a minimum and jewellery, other than watches or wedding rings, should not be worn. Hair had to be short or tied back and secured in a hair net. Ponytails were not acceptable, so most police women wore their hair in a bun at the nape of the neck.

Other equipment included handcuffs and a whistle. As personal radios were just coming into use, I never used my whistle other than when, as part of my police duties, I helped out at a school sports day, but the chain added a bit of ornament to the uniform.

At that time male officers were issued with a fifteen-inch long wooden truncheon, which was kept in a specially designed trouser pocket. As women didn't wear trousers, we didn't get a truncheon and were no doubt supposed to use our feminine charms to get out of trouble. A few years later, women were issued with a little six-inch truncheon to keep in our handbags and you can imagine the crude jokes, which accompanied them.

Now, suitably equipped, I duly pressed my uniforms and bulled my shoes to the best of my ability. The art of 'spit and polish' was new to me and something that I would learn to perfect in the months to come. Once the preparatory work had been done, our small band of new recruits, was duly inspected, first by the training staff, and then by an Inspector, before we were pronounced ready for training school.

Before receiving a warrant card we were taken to the local Magistrate's Court to be sworn in as Constables. This involved swearing an oath of allegiance to the Queen. We were required to raise our right hand while holding the New Testament and read the words:

'I do solemnly and sincerely declare and affirm that I will well and truly serve our Sovereign Lady, the Queen, in the office of Constable, without favour or affection, malice or ill will; and that I will, to the best of my power, cause the peace to be kept and preserved, and prevent all offences against the persons and properties of Her Majesty's subjects and that while I continue to hold the said office I will, to the best of my skill and knowledge, discharge all the duties thereof faithfully according to law'

I had never previously given evidence or even been inside a court, so felt quite nervous, but very proud to be making this commitment. The Magistrate then handed us our warrant cards, congratulated us on becoming Constables and told us to wear our uniforms proudly, as we were about to do a very important job for society.

I became Woman Police Constable No.4 Mitchell and after training would be stationed at Greyfriars Police Station in Bedford.

On leaving the courthouse, we were quickly brought back down to ground, as the Training Sergeant said that we were to put our warrant cards in a safe place, but not to attempt to use them or the associated police powers until after we had completed our initial training course. There was a long way to go before we became Constables in the practical sense.

During the induction training, we were not required to do any physical training, but were advised to keep ourselves fit, ready for training school. In those days there was no initial physical fitness test that required strength and stamina. It seemed that certification by the police doctor that a recruit had four limbs, a working heart and lungs, was sufficient to meet initial Force requirements. I certainly felt fit and well and was happily complacent, believing that I would cope with whatever training school had in store for me.

As new recruits, we attended a number of classroom sessions where we were taught Force policy, geography, boundaries, rank structure and organisation. We were also issued a booklet of 'Police Definitions' which we were advised to start learning by heart. It included police powers, wondrous things such as diseases of animals, liquor licensing times, and numerous other miscellaneous pieces of legislation, which at the time appeared to be superfluous. I could not then imagine that this little book would later become the equivalent of a holy mantra.

There wasn't an immediate place for me at training school, but I had been appointed early for budgetary reasons. The new financial year for public services began on 1st April and any under spend could not be carried forward. No doubt, senior officers had to make a choice between purchasing half a dozen new filing cabinets or appointing another constable, and I won! Whilst waiting to attend training school, I was given appropriate jobs to usefully occupy my time.

One of the HQ civilian telephonists went sick, leaving a shortfall in the switchboard room. Someone decided that this was a suitable occupation for a female recruit and I was duly allocated this duty. The remaining switchboard operator had been in this role for many years and was clearly highly proficient. She did her patient best to explain to me the vagaries of the enormous private branch exchange (PBX) switchboard, which connected headquarters with all the other police stations within the

Force. I think I understood the theory of it, but was slow in picking up the practical implications. The board had at least two hundred connections to extensions both at HQ and on divisional stations (minimal by today's standards). A numbered disc on the board identified each extension and would click up and down to indicate a caller waiting. The operator then used one of the many retractable cords and plugs on the board to connect to that line and a corresponding cord to an outside extension. At all times, the operator's voice would be calm, polite, concise and helpful. Everyone was addressed as 'Sir' or 'Madam' and the aim was to keep the communications running efficiently. When making a connection, the operator lifted a switch that allowed her to speak to and hear both parties, and once they were connected, she was supposed to drop the switch, leaving them in private conversation. I was given the impression that 'listening in' was absolutely against the rules, so it was a mystery to me how switchboard operators always seemed to know everyone's business. I was given my first practical lesson during a quiet time, and under the watchful eye of the switchboard operator. I managed to put the right plugs into the right holes, but I was slow as I did not know the names of key individuals or who worked in which department, so had to use the printed reference sheets. Nonetheless, my trainer was happy that I had got the gist of the job and when one o'clock arrived she announced that she was going for her lunch break and was sure that I would be OK.

Although a little apprehensive, I felt honoured to be left in such a vital position. It was about fifteen minutes before all hell let loose. It seemed that every disc on the board was flashing madly and I had used all available cords, which were now like well-mixed spaghetti. Remaining unused cords simply wouldn't reach the vacant holes. I lost track of which switch to put up or down and left crossed open lines, so that people were talking to each other throughout the

Force. Occasionally I tried to explain what was going on and found some people patient and understanding, but others were very rude and aggressive. I was in a rising state of panic, with sweating palms, an increased heart rate and flushed face. I felt very alone in the switchboard room, which resembled a claustrophobic cupboard at the best of times, and hoped that it would not be long before the regular operator returned. Then, my challenge came to a head, when the disc marked number one, belonging to the Chief Constable, started to click up and down. I knew that he was to be given priority at all times, so I made an instant decision. I pulled out every other plug on the board, put all the switches down and then plugged into the Chief's extension. I calmly said, "Good afternoon Sir. Can I help you?" I then ensured that his call went smoothly, before responding to some of the other wildly flashing discs. It seemed that for the entire hour, communication within the Force was literally 'haywire' and 'that silly bitch on switchboard' was the topic of many a conversation. When the switchboard operator returned, I explained the situation and then gratefully went for my break while she sorted out any remaining problems. I was never asked to do switchboard duty again and just hoped that I would make a better job of being a policewoman.

I was then assigned duties in the Fingerprint (FP) Department at Police HQ. In those days there were no computerised files, so all recording, classifying and checking was a painstaking manual task, carried out by fingerprint experts. Fingerprints were taken from crime scenes and from suspects for investigation purposes. They were also taken from victims of crime and from police officers for elimination purposes. All these fingerprint forms were then submitted to the FP Department, where they were carefully cross-checked to identify offenders and collate evidence for court proceedings. I found this work both informative and fascinating, as it was an important part of traditional crime detection. I learned that fingerprinting dates back to Victorian times, when Henry Faulds developed the 'Henry Classification System' based on loops, whorls and arches and a Fingerprint Bureau was established at Scotland Yard. Later in my career, I would find that this system would be highly influential in the formation of the modern Automated Fingerprint Identification System (AFIS) and biometric services. As a new recruit, I was happy to be doing something useful and learning something about real detective work. After only a few weeks in the FP Department, I was informed that I had been found a place at Ryton on Dunsmore District Training Centre. I was excited, but knew that there would be challenging times ahead.

Chapter 2

Training School

On Monday 14th April, my parents drove me up to Ryton on Dunsmore in Warwickshire to start the thirteen- week police initial training course. Until now, I had lived at home with my parents, so I felt like a nervous child going to school for the first time. The training centre did nothing to improve my morale. Ryton was an old Royal Air Force Camp and on this dull day, looked dreary, grey and inhospitable.

I didn't want my parents to be aware of my apprehension or to kiss me goodbye in front of fellow officers, so I asked them to drop me and all my baggage, at the main entrance. I bade them a cheery farewell and strode off towards the main door.

I went into the reception area, where a male Sergeant was checking in several new male recruits. He was efficient and abrupt as he checked individual's names off his sheet. He asked me my name, rank, number and Force, read a few details and then said, "I see you were a Special Constable". I replied "Yes, Sergeant" and felt a glimmer of hope that my three years of voluntary service would stand me in good stead. He looked me straight in the eyes and said "Well you can forget all that. You'll learn to be a real police officer here". The Woman Sergeant then showed me to my room in the female quarters, where I was to unpack, change into uniform and then meet the other recruits for coffee in the canteen.

I was relieved to find that I had my own room rather than a dormitory, as I had never had to share a bedroom. The room was small, but reasonably warm and equipped with a bed, bedside cabinet, wardrobe, desk and chair. There was a wash basin, but the shared showers and toilets were down the corridor. Ever since school, I have hated communal showers and really value my privacy, so was glad to see that at least there were shower cubicles with curtains.

The Woman Sergeant told me that all uniform and equipment was to be put away and only three items, such as alarm clock, radio and clothes brush would remain on show. The bed linen was neatly stacked on the bed and I was dismayed to find that there was a yellow coloured candlewick bedspread. I had already learned that fluff is the biggest enemy of dark uniforms, so wondered why we had this additional challenge. I would soon learn how to make my bed in regulation style and then each morning to strip the bed and make a bed pack. Some recruits soon decided to keep their bed pack intact and sleep under the bedspread, thereby saving ten minutes in the morning routine.

After unpacking I wandered along the corridor and on hearing voices, knocked on one of the other doors. I was greeted by two cheerful young ladies, with Welsh accents, who had joined the same Force and travelled to Ryton together. Most of our intake would be officers from the West Midlands and Welsh Forces, but I was the only officer from Bedfordshire, so was determined to make friends. After preliminary introductions, the three of us headed over to the canteen to meet the rest of our intake. There was lively chatter going on as we all checked out the other new recruits. Then, the Sergeants came in and we fell into an expectant silence as they began to call out our names. We were divided into classes, introduced to our training Sergeants and then formally addressed by the Commandant, who was head of the regional training centre. There were twenty-two new recruits in my class, sixteen male police constables (PCs) and six women police constables (WPCs). After classroom familiarisation, briefing on the rules and regulations and the issue of a timetable, we had lunch. Then it was time to change into physical training (PT) kit and report to the gymnasium. I had never been slim and athletic, but was fairly active and fitter than many of my female friends at home, so felt that I would cope with whatever was expected of me. I had noticed that most of the other female recruits were quite slim, whereas I was a curvaceous size fourteen. When we arrived in the gym, we were told to stand in lines and step up to the front when called. I soon discovered that, to complete the records, the two Sergeants, one male and one female, were recording our height, weight and chest measurement. One Sergeant held the tape measure and shouted out the figures while the other recorded.

Each time a woman stepped forward, the Woman Sergeant wielded the tape measure and carried out the measurements, which were then audible to everyone in the room. Even with the tailor at HQ, I had been quite shy, so this was a bit of a trial, which I knew I must face with a nonchalant air. I stepped forward and had my height and weight recorded and then came the dreaded tape measure. The Sergeant said "Breathe out. Breathe in. Hold your breath" She then called out thirty-six exhaled, thirty eight inhaled and there was a sudden cheer from the male officers. I returned to my place, conscious of their amused grins and my own rather red face. The humiliation may not have been intended, but I certainly felt it and realised that I would have to toughen up.

Training school was a real shock to my system. Training involved military style discipline, constant drills, classroom based learning of law and definitions, physical training (PT), self-defence, practical scenarios, first aid and lifesaving.

Full uniform had to be worn each day, and each morning began with recruits lined up on the parade square for inspection. It was a team effort to brush each other down before parade, so we all carried either a small clothes brush or a roll of sticky tape to clear away any fluff. If one member of our class was less than perfect, the Drill Sergeant would punish the whole class with extra drill practice, so we soon learned to work together,

After inspection, we learned the basics of marching. I say 'basics' as initially some officers seemed to have difficulty knowing their left foot from their right or being able to swing their arms in unison with the opposite leg. The Drill Sergeant soon let us know of his displeasure, if anyone got out of step. Each class had its own appointed 'drill pig', usually an ex-military man, who would run remedial sessions as required.

I had been a Girl Guide and a Land Ranger, so I at least had a head start when it came to marching and found that this was something I really enjoyed.

As the weeks progressed and our marching improved, band music was played over the loudspeakers and we optimistically prepared for our passing-out parade. We marched in unison and then split into classes, criss-crossing on the parade square.

The real party piece was when, wearing pristine white gloves, we learned traffic signals to music. This was fun to learn and hopefully would impress visitors to the passing-out parade, but would prove to be useless when later sorting out traffic jams at busy road junctions!

We also learned to make bed packs, bull shoes and press uniforms to a sharp crease. There were all sorts of tricks to be learned like using brown paper under the iron to get sharp creases without shiny marks, or putting a line of candle wax inside the trouser crease. Like most of the WPCs, I traded skills with male colleagues, often ironing or sewing in exchange for bulling shoes. Ex-military officers were in great demand, as we all learned the art of 'spit and polish' in an almost ritual fashion. The lid of the polish tin was filled with warm water; a soft duster was moulded around the index finger and dipped in polish and then slowly worked in circles on the shoe leather. Spit was added to the polish and gradually a 'bulled' area appeared. When properly executed, the toe-caps became like mirrors and we could literally see our faces in them. Some experts propounded the art of warming the polish with a candle flame to achieve the final gloss, but I didn't try this as I saw someone set fire to their shoes. I was shocked and embarrassed one day when a burly West Midlands officer asked me if I had a sanitary towel that he could have. When he saw the expression on my face, he explained that they were made of very soft cotton and made really good polishing cloths, using the loops as handles. The old fashioned type of sanitary towel had loops to attach to an elastic belt, but I thought that it was only women who knew about such items. I was probably a bit of a prude and would never have discussed such things with my father or brothers, so felt very uncomfortable with this conversation. I mumbled a negative reply and gratefully kept my head down, concentrating on my own polishing method.

There was a small shop at the training school that sold essential items such as boot polish, dusters, clothes brushes, toiletries, sweets and shoes. I bought myself a pair of shoes with rigid toe-caps, as I soon learned that soft leather shoes creased and ruined the high shine. We all kept one pair of highly polished shoes wrapped in a soft towel or pillow-case, ready for drill and inspection and wore another pair for everyday use. It was a cardinal sin to accidentally stand on another officer's toe-caps.

If time permitted, once the studying, ironing and bulling of shoes was done, we were able to enjoy some social time in the student bar until 10.45 pm, as 'lights out' was at 11pm. We all dressed in civilian clothes in the evenings and the women received lots of attention from our male colleagues. I don't remember any sexist behaviour, but just good-natured banter and flattery. When it was time to leave, some of the men would walk the women back to their accommodation, but had to stop when they reached the sign saying 'No men beyond this point'. Amorous couples who wanted to snatch a good night kiss tended to line up in front of the sign until the duty squad came along and moved them on. We all took our turn as part of the duty squad, so none of us ever gave our colleagues a hard time,

The Woman Sergeant used to patrol around the female block after 11 pm to ensure that we were all safely tucked up in bed alone! To be honest, I think most of us were too shattered to think about extramural activities and just wanted a good night's sleep before the challenges of the next day.

We studied every aspect of criminal law applicable to general policing, and learned legal definitions parrot fashion, for example definitions of theft, burglary and assault, powers of arrest and what constituted a road traffic accident. Each Monday there was a written definition test with marks deducted for any mistakes. This was important, as all our test and exam marks were recorded as part of the overall course assessment, which ultimately led to passing or failing the Initial Training Course.

We also learned more obscure subjects such as diseases of animals and sexual offences such as incest and bestiality. I realised that I was very naive and during the lesson on sexual offences, I commented that I had never heard of bestiality. A male colleague tried to help out by saying "You know Welsh farmers, sheep and wellies". I still didn't understand, so when I was next home, I asked my older brother to explain, which he delighted in doing. I'll leave the explanation to your imagination! I was shocked that such things happened in any society, but hoped that I wouldn't have to deal with anything like that when I returned to my Force.

In addition to written exams, there were practical exercises in dealing with incidents such as road traffic accidents, drunken brawls or making arrests. There were also constant drills and physical fitness tests in swimming, lifesaving and self-defence.

Female recruits were prime targets for ridicule and discipline by the Physical Training Instructor (PTI) and Drill Sergeant. Ex-military officers were held in high esteem, but ex Special Constables were ripe for ridicule. I remember one occasion when we were lined up for inspection by the Drill Sergeant. When he walked down the line and got to me, he stared at my face and said "Are you wearing makeup, woman?" I replied "Just some mascara Sergeant". He then shouted "Get off my parade square and wash that muck off your face woman. At the double!" Feeling really humiliated, I rushed to the nearest bathroom to wash my face. I wasn't aware that wearing a little mascara was against the rules, but I had learned that no one argued with the Drill Sergeant.

Some women disappeared early in the course, either failing the physical fitness tests or simply hating the military style discipline. One young lady made her escape by hitching a lift in the bread delivery van at 7am and was never seen again!

My real hate was the Wednesday afternoon three or five mile cross-country around the quarry at Ryton, which was often wet and muddy. I hate cross-country and I hate mud, so detested this exhausting but obligatory challenge. I realised that we all needed to be physically and mentally fit to make good police officers, but I failed to appreciate the significance of cross-country running. After all, the modern police service had cars and helicopters, so why did I need to run five miles? I was reasonably fit, an excellent swimmer and a good team player. My girls' grammar school education had taught me to enjoy sport, but I wasn't a natural runner and cross-country had always been an opportunity to catch up on the latest gossip, while undertaking a slow jog. Besides which, I had noticed that all good female runners were small-breasted and slim-hipped and I was neither. Nonetheless, my philosophy at training school had to be to do my best at everything.

On the day of the first cross-country we had lessons in the morning and then went to the canteen for lunch. As I stood in the self-service queue, I chatted to the other girls in my class and suggested that we support each other by keeping a steady pace during the cross-country. It was only then that I realised that I must be a bit slow, mentally I mean. Two of the girls were non-swimmers and had somehow been granted additional swimming lessons. One girl was complaining of bad period pains and another said that she had sprained her ankle and would be helping our class Sergeant with some of his duties. It seemed that I was to be the only female participating in the cross-country run. My appetite disappeared and I could only manage a bowl of soup before the bell went to summon us to the afternoon sessions. I turned up at the gymnasium wearing what I considered to be very decent, sensible gym kit, consisting of navy hockey shorts (divided skirt style) and a blue aertex polo shirt. The PTI lined us all up for inspection. On reaching me he shouted "What the hell are you wearing woman?" Without waiting for an answer, he shouted "Follow me" and strode off towards the gym store. There, he rummaged in a box and found a pair of bright orange running shorts and a white aertex top, which he then threw at me. They were creased and smelled of stale sweat, but worse still they both looked a bit on the small side. He shouted, "Well don't just stand there staring. Go and get changed!" I said "I don't want to wear these and in any case I don't think that they will fit". He seemed to sneer at me and then shouted "Do as you are damn well told woman if you want to survive this course. Get kitted-out and make it quick!" I felt my face turning red with anger and exasperation, but realised that this was no time to argue. Sex discrimination was a term unheard of in 1969, the police service philosophy being 'if you can't stand the heat get out of the fire'. I reluctantly went and changed. The T-shirt was ridiculously tight and accentuated my figure and the orange shorts were high cut and seemed quite indecent to me. I turned up, my face now glowing red with embarrassment and this was not helped by the audible sniggers of some of the men. The PTI then screamed at me "When I blow the first whistle, woman, you start running. When I blow the second whistle the men will run and keep her running ahead of you by whatever means you like". This was in my view total humiliation and I could feel the tears welling up in my eyes. Perspiration was running off me even before we started running. From that moment on, I hated the PTI, but vowed to myself that he would not know my feelings or see me cry.

The whistle blew and I set off along the muddy track that led around the quarry adjacent to the training centre. Within minutes, the second whistle blew and twenty or so men set off behind me. I felt very anxious, as I didn't want to make a fool of myself or show any weakness. Although these men were friends and colleagues, I was aware that the PTI had pointed out that I was different and given them a task to perform. Maybe his aggressive, sexist attitude would affect this group of otherwise very reasonable, friendly men. I could hear their voices and the pounding of feet behind me and I began to have some understanding of how a fox felt when it first heard the baying of hounds during a hunt. Just to make matters worse, I noticed that it had started to rain heavily and puddles were quickly forming on the muddy path. I was determined to keep running and get through this experience without cracking. I began to concentrate on just keeping a steady pace, but I could hear my own heavy breathing and the pounding of my heart, not to mention squelching of my gym shoes in the mud. Then, suddenly, I became aware of two of the men running alongside me. One said "Don't worry about the PTI. He obviously doesn't like WPCs, but don't let him crack you" I felt a real sense of relief and managed to thank them for their support. We all then saved our breath for the run and I was grateful just to finish.

On another occasion when we set off on the cross-country run, two of the men came up with a marvellous suggestion. Instead of going around the quarry, we could take a short cut down a steep path across the middle, saving a mile and surfacing on the path at the other side. I readily agreed and like three naughty children, we laughed as we stumbled down the steep path and stopped to rest amongst the huge boulders of hewn rock. After a brief rest and a social chat, we were off again, this time climbing up a steep incline to reach the path, where we joined the leaders and ran the last half-mile back to the training centre. The PTI was waiting for us at the finishing line and checking off our names as we shouted them out. I felt triumphant and even managed a grin, hoping that he was impressed that I was with the leaders.

We all went to our accommodation blocks to shower and change ready for the evening meal. I luxuriated in a long, hot shower, using perfumed shampoo and shower gel to make me feel relaxed and feminine again. The steam eased the aches and pains and I began to feel quite exhilarated. We had permission to wear civilian clothes to attend the evening meal after a sports afternoon, so I decided to make a special effort. I dressed in smart, feminine clothes, paid attention to my make-up and wore my favourite perfume. On arriving in the canteen, several of my colleagues complimented me on how nice I looked. I began to think that perhaps the run had been worth it in order to realise the friendship and win the respect of my colleagues.

I ate heartily, tucking in to steak and kidney pie, followed by jam roly-poly and a liberal amount of hot, sweet custard. I figured that I had earned a good meal. I intended to have a restful evening, pressing my uniform, bulling my shoes and then lying on my bed studying.

The meal ended and we all waited for any formal address by the Commandant or any notices from staff before we left the dining hall. As the PTI walked onto the platform I had a strange sinking feeling in the pit of my stomach, although this may have just been the jam roly-poly hitting home. The PTI then announced the names of three people who were to stand up. To my horror, I heard my name called and I rose wearily to my feet. "These three students failed to check in at the half-way point on the cross country. They will report to the gymnasium in full kit in fifteen minutes to repeat the run." One of my fellow offenders said "Come on love, we'd better be going. Don't let the bastard get you down."

The repeat run was for me purgatory. I had eaten too much and was violently sick after the first half-mile. It was now getting dark, cold, and the rain felt like icy needles. Worse still, the PTI ran with us and was able to witness my agony. We were only on the short route but this was the longest three miles of my life. When I finally returned to my room, I was totally exhausted, and smelled of sweat, vomit and mud. Alone at last, I burst out crying. I wanted so much to be a police officer, but found some aspects of training school very hard. This did not bear any relation to what I had been doing as a special constable and I began to wonder if I had made a big mistake. Somehow, I found the reserves that I needed, pulled myself together, went for a shower and then literally fell into my bed. I was determined not to quit, as I knew that once initial training was over that I would get back to real policing, the job that I loved. Tomorrow would be a new day with new challenges.

The final weeks of training consisted of exams, assessed practical scenarios, a mock courtroom and physical fitness tests.

We all had our own strengths and weaknesses, so whenever possible, we helped each other to achieve. I enjoyed the swimming and lifesaving sessions, but realised that some of my colleagues, particularly the non – swimmers, dreaded these sessions. Everyone was expected to overcome their fears, jump into the pool and learn to swim. When it came to the lifesaving test, I was paired up with a very weak swimmer, who told me that he was terrified. First of all he acted as the drowning person, while I saved him, but I don't think that he had to roleplay too much. Then came his turn to save me and I became aware that instead of holding my chin to support me, he was simply hanging on for dear life! I told him to hang on and whenever the examiner wasn't watching, I gave a few powerful kicks with my legs and eventually got us to the edge of the pool. He then managed to haul himself and me out of the water and put me in the recovery position. He passed the test and whispered "Thanks, I owe you a drink later".

I may not have excelled as an athlete, but I did work very hard at my studies and won the top student award. I was presented with a set of 'Baker & Wilkie Police Promotion Handbooks', which would later encourage me to study further.

Having successfully passed all the required academic and physical tests, we all looked forward to our Passing-Out Parade, which would formally mark the end of our initial training. Although I had not appreciated the value of some of the militaristic traditions imposed on police training, I did understand the importance of this final parade. We had all arrived at Ryton as individuals from various backgrounds, with our own set of values. In twelve weeks we had become a disciplined unit, part of the police family and with a shared culture. The thin blue line was still predominately a 'brotherhood', but I and my female colleagues had survived the initiation and like threads, would be woven into the fabric of the organisation.

Friday 11th July 1969 was the final day of our course and I felt very proud when we marched before parents, invited guests and dignitaries at our Passing-Out parade. It was a day of mixed emotions as we marched in unison, celebrated with glee and then parted from our friends to begin our careers. Training school had not been easy, but I had learned a great deal, was a stronger person and better prepared to deal with the challenges of routine policing. My colleagues and I returned to our respective Police Forces to start two years as Probationer Constables.

Chapter 3

Women's Work

I was very happy to be posted to Greyfriars Po̱l: Station, Bedford, as I felt back on home territory and in my comfort zone. Training school had merely been the preliminary and the real work and learning was about to begin.

All women officers worked in the Policewomen's Department under the guidance of a Woman Sergeant. We dealt mainly with missing persons and offences involving women and children. There were two sections, each comprised of six policewomen and a Woman Sergeant. We usually worked a seven and a half hour day or evening shift. Male officers worked eight-hour shifts, so we were paid seven eighths of the men's pay. Regulations required us to go off duty by 11pm, unless it was our turn to be on call-out duty as matron. This required us to go into the police station to search or supervise women prisoners, or take a statement from a victim of a sexual offence.

I didn't have a telephone in my flat and mobile phones didn't exist in those days so, if I was on call and required at the police station, the area patrol officer would call round and then drive me back to the police station. When I lived in my first bedsit, the officer would have to wait outside, but once I got my own council flat, I could be more hospitable and invite a colleague in for coffee, while I got changed into uniform ready for duty. I was very trusting of my male colleagues and certainly never felt compromised as they all behaved like gentlemen.

On arriving at the police station, the duty Sergeant would brief me on the duty requirement. Taking a statement from a victim of rape could take many hours and then it was necessary to organise a medical examination.

The on-call policewoman started by taking basic details and if a suspect was likely to be at large, a description would be circulated over the radio. A detective would be allocated the investigation and was usually at the police station waiting for sufficient information to start the investigation or make an early arrest. Needless to say, there was great pressure on the policewoman to conduct the interview and obtain a statement as soon as possible. Victims were sometimes hysterical, traumatised, drunk or for various reasons, non-communicative, so it was difficult work. It was necessary to ask lots of pertinent questions to establish the facts and on occasions, the woman concerned would decide to withdraw the complaint. A statement of withdrawal would then be taken and handed to the waiting Detective, who was usually very grateful to be able to record the incident as 'no crime'. We did our best to be sensitive and caring, but obtaining evidence always seemed to be paramount and in retrospect, I realise that we had a great deal to learn about victim handling and support. I would go on to witness and sometimes pioneer improvements in this area.

If a female prisoner had been brought into the police station and was staying in custody overnight, I would have to stay until another policewoman came on duty at 8 am.

All prisoners had to be searched before being placed in a cell and if suspected of a drugs offence, a strip search was required. It had to be thorough, because there was always the possibility of the prisoner having a weapon or taking drugs whilst in custody, or hiding such items in the cell.

31

Although I always tried to act very professional and matter of fact about doing the search, I really disliked this duty. I had far too much empathy with some of the prisoners, as I know that I would have found a strip search very demeaning. This was not the case with violent or drunk prisoners, as it was often such a struggle to search them that I lost all empathy. We had disposable gloves to wear, but it was still a very unpleasant job, especially if the prisoner had wet or soiled themselves, or vomited on their clothing.

The police officer conducting the search would then sign the custody record and record any property found on the prisoner. It was a disciplinary offence of neglect of duty to fail to properly search a prisoner, as possession of drugs or an offensive weapon could later lead to the prisoner harming themselves or injuring a police officer.

There were no toilets or wash basins in the cells in those days, so if a prisoner wanted to go to the toilet, they had to ring the bell in their cell. The policewoman would then escort the prisoner to the toilet and washroom at the end of the cellblock and wait at a discreet distance. If there were a number of female prisoners in custody, it could be a busy night!

The policewoman acting as matron would be allowed to rest in the matron's room, which was near to the cell block. Some of my female colleagues managed to sleep but, even if I had been on duty all day, I never felt able to take advantage of this situation. I'm a light sleeper and could hear all the noise in the corridor outside and was very aware that I could be called at any time. The night section station staff always had tea and coffee brewing, so I would use caffeine to keep me awake and help out in the control room or enquiry office until required in the cells.

Policewomen on call out didn't get paid overtime, but did get time off in lieu of the hours worked. Sometimes I would save up those hours to enable me to enjoy a long weekend break, but more often I used my extra time to catch up on sleep.

Generally speaking, I did not find police work too physically demanding, but the irregular hours did sometimes put one's body clock out of kilter and lead to sleep disturbance. Being involved in a struggle with a prisoner, a car chase, or a fight on the street was just a part of the job. It was exciting rather than frightening and certainly got the adrenaline flowing, so that all officers involved would be on a bit of a high later and enjoy an informal debrief over a drink in the bar.

There was one occasional duty that I found both physically and mentally tiring, as it was very much in the public arena. When starting at 8am, one of the policewomen could be detailed to do traffic control at the road junction between Prebend Street and Cauldwell Street, known as 'Black Diamond' or at St. Mary's junction. There were traffic lights at both of these junctions, but when detailed to carry out traffic control from 8am – 9am, we took a key to turn off the lights and direct traffic manually. Wearing a fluorescent tabard and white gauntlet style gloves, the officer would step out into the middle of the very busy junction with cars, lorries and buses passing in dangerously close proximity. The traffic noise and fumes were all enveloping, but you had to keep a clear head and direct traffic not just on the two main roads, but also control the filter lanes. Bearing in mind that at training school I had learned traffic signals to music while lines of marching police officers crossed ranks, the real thing was initially quite terrifying. I never really understood the purpose of this traffic control duty, as in my opinion traffic moved more freely by relying on the traffic lights rather than an officer acting like a windmill in the centre of the road. Nonetheless, once allocated the duty, I simply followed orders and got on with the job. The mental concentration and upper arm exercise was rather like a combination of playing chess, while doing aerobics and it always gave me a healthy appetite when it came to refreshment time.

During the day shifts, when the Women Sergeants were on duty, the policewomen tended to sit together in the canteen at refreshment breaks. During the evening shifts, however, whilst working with a male section, we would tend to join our male colleagues in the canteen. Breaks were in two shifts, each for three quarters of an hour, if the exigencies of duty allowed. We would all rush in, eat our sandwiches or order a 'chips with everything' canteen meal. All food was consumed as quickly as possible, because if the radio or loudspeaker went we would all go rushing out to a fight or the next job. If it remained peaceful, we would all play snooker, cards or table tennis. These games were one of the highlights of section life on the traditional eight-hour shift pattern (Earlies: 6am – 2pm, Lates: 2pm – 10pm or Nights: 10pm – 6am.) Whatever the hour, we seemed to eat the same greasy food, drink steaming mugs of tea or coffee and enjoy working and playing as a team. There was sexist banter directed at WPCs, but in those days it wasn't recognised as such. We all laughed at each other's trials and weaknesses, but we knew that when the chips were down that our colleagues would be there to support us. It was this camaraderie that made the job seem special and like being part of a big family.

As young single policewomen, our accommodation was selected and approved by the Woman Sergeant, as regulations said that we should live in a place of good repute, preferably with a 'homely family'. Our moral welfare was carefully scrutinised by the Women Sergeants, who gave us very firm advice if they felt that we were associating with the wrong people, or not behaving in a professional manner.

I was found a bedsit room on the upper floor of a Victorian house in Park Avenue, Bedford. All residents were female and no male visitors were allowed in the house after 10 pm. The landlord kept a careful watch and there were gravel paths surrounding the house. It seems that he could hear the slightest crunching noise on the gravel and would appear instantly to check out any visitors and inform the Woman Sergeant if there was any inappropriate activity! As I had previously lived with my parents and was not used to a high degree of independence, I accepted this regime for my first two years and found it rather like joining a new family.

If we wanted to move home it had to be vetted by a supervisor. Boyfriends were also checked out and we had to formally apply in writing to the Chief Constable if we wished to get engaged or marry. That was a step forward though from the early days of policewomen when they had to be single or widows.

I found police work fulfilling and tiring, so I did not miss not having a steady relationship. It was the norm following a late shift for the entire section to meet at the police station bar for a few drinks after work. The bar was located on the fourth floor of the police station, adjacent to the canteen and was run by a civilian bar steward. It was the scene of many a celebration, but also the place where we wound down after a particularly difficult or harrowing shift. There was no formal stress counselling in those days, so this was often the only outlet for our feelings. Black humour certainly played a part, but this was where we came together as a family and offered support when it was needed. If a job had been well done, the Inspector would usually buy the drinks and congratulate everyone.

The real party spirit came to the forefront on our long weekends, when most members of the section would take their wives, partners and friends to the police club located at the Bedford Athletic Club stadium in Newnham Avenue,

Bedford. We had use of the upper floor, which had a dance floor and bar. I'm not sure of the financial arrangements, but our club events were run by a Sergeant and PC from Bedford, who regularly gave their own time, but occasionally excused themselves from other duties to organise events at the club. They were both excellent DJs, but also arranged live bands and other entertainment. I rarely missed one of the big events at the club, as it was an opportunity to let our hair down and dance the night away in a safe environment.

Bedfordshire Police also held an Annual Police Ball at the Corn Exchange in St. Paul's Square, Bedford. It was a stylish affair and for ladies it was an opportunity to wear a ball gown and feel like a princess for the evening, escorted by a gentleman in evening dress. In my early years of policing I only went once, as I couldn't afford a ticket or a ball gown and didn't have a 'Prince Charming' to take me. Instead, I used to call in on duty and enjoy free food and drink given by the catering staff. The top table was always occupied by the Chief Constable, senior officers and local dignitaries, and this was probably the first time that I had seen them in relaxed, social mode. When the meal and speeches were finished, there was dancing until 1am and then official cars and taxis turned up to take everyone home. By then, I was usually round the corner in the High Street helping to sort out the drunks emerging from other premises in a far less civilised manner!

The social life within the police service was so good that I soon found that most of my friends were police colleagues and I had little time for life outside the police service. Occasionally, I would go to the cinema or clubbing with Ann, the girl who occupied the next room to me at my lodgings. Ann was also in her early twenties and worked in an office. She was beautiful, had a model like figure and was very charming, but in no way conceited. I enjoyed her company and we became good friends, sometimes spending our evenings in each other's rooms. Having a friend outside the police service meant that I could forget my job for a while and indulge in girlie things for a change. We were both short of cash after we had paid the rent and bought our food, so sometimes we would pool resources as a treat. Soup, beans on toast and a few glasses of cheap sherry was our idea of a banquet!

Ann and I went shopping together one Saturday and saw some cheap fur jackets for sale in the market. We had both been paid so decided to treat ourselves. Ann bought a dark brown jacket and I bought a lovely honey coloured jacket. That evening we dressed in our new fur jackets and went out to a club in town, where ladies got free entry before 10 pm. We were approached by two very presentable, smartly dressed men, wearing dark suits, collar and ties. They bought us drinks and we spent the evening in their company. During conversation they asked us what our jobs were and I told them that I was a librarian, as I really didn't want to get into the inevitable discussions about speeding tickets or drink driving. They later walked us home to Park Avenue. We couldn't invite them in, so stood under the street lamp for a kiss and cuddle. On saying 'Good night' we backed away and hurried into our lodgings, but then both roared with laughter. We had both noticed that our new fur jackets had moulted and left a layer of fur on the men's dark suits, leaving them looking like a pair of Yetis. The jackets turned out to be made of Coney, or rabbit fur, and were clearly not the bargains that we had thought. Strangely enough, we never saw our suitors again!

I subsequently introduced Ann to my brother Peter, who was in the Royal Air Force, but came home on leave. They made a handsome couple and, after he had 'crunched the gravel' on a few occasions, they got engaged and she eventually became my sister-in-law.

On my days off I would often go home to my parent's house in Biggleswade and my mother would make sure that I was properly fed. We didn't talk a great deal about my job, but my mother did say that she worried about some of the risks involved. I did my best to reassure them and they knew that I was very happy in the police service. In the early days they never told me that they were proud of me, but I was pleased to see that they had a framed photo of me in uniform in a prominent position

Bearing in mind that this was 1969, the style of policing was still traditional, but things were changing. The TV series Dixon of Dock Green was still running until 1976, but Z Cars was now also reflecting a more aggressive policing culture. There was no doubt that the public still preferred the idea of the traditional 'Bobby on the beat', but on the other hand they expected a speedy response when a crime was committed. Chief Constables were trying to find an effective compromise and Bedfordshire Chief Constable, Henry Pratt had introduced unit beat policing throughout the force area. The number of local beat officers was reduced and most male officers now patrolled in "Panda" cars on a twenty-four hour basis. Bedfordshire panda cars were a fleet of minis, but we also had additional Vauxhall Vivas for use by CID and other specialist departments. The cars all had radios fitted and patrol officers also had personal radios so for the first time there was mobile communication throughout the Force. A new radio control room was established at police headquarters.

The policewomen's department had an unmarked Vauxhall Viva, but initially I was unable to drive it as I hadn't had a police driving course, so either had to walk or ask for lifts to jobs. Although I had passed my civilian driving test at the age of eighteen years, I didn't have my own car so was still a very inexperienced driver.

In November 1969, I was allocated a four week standard driving course and reported to Bedfordshire police driving school in Kempston. I was now twenty-two years of age, but still limited in driving experience. I felt quite nervous, whereas my two male colleagues on the course seemed much more competent and confident. Our instructor known as 'Fangio' after an Italian racing driver, soon identified that he had two experienced male drivers and one rather timid female in his car. He put us through our paces, learning the art of 'double-declutching' and driving safely at speed.

As I was wearing a skirt, stockings and suspenders and felt under close scrutiny when it was my time to drive, I was very conscious of not letting my skirt ride up above my knees showing my stocking tops. I remember Fangio saying "For God's sake woman stop trying to drive a car with your knees together!" There was a muffled snigger from my two male colleagues. I eventually learned to relax even if I knew the instructor was getting quite an eyeful!

Towards the end of the course we hit the open road driving to Devizes in Wiltshire, while the instructor assessed each of us for part of the journey. We had to give a running commentary describing the terrain, road junctions, speed and appropriate gear changes, which demonstrated our ability to think ahead. This requires a high degree of concentration and I was always exhausted at the end of the day. I passed the course and was delighted to be authorised to drive police vehicles.

As policewomen, we liaised with all sections but were very much a separate department, primarily dealing with missing persons and offences involving women and children. These included rape, incest and other sexual offences, child abuse, domestic violence and schools liaison. Our roles generally dealt with the seamier side of life and although most of us were fairly young and naïve, we all had to learn not to appear shocked by anything we saw or heard. We all attended a policewomen's course, where we learned to deal with a wide range of sexual offences and the finer art of taking victims' statements. This was much more helpful and informative than the lessons on sexual offences at training school, as it was easier to ask questions within an all-female environment.

As a fairly naive young woman, I also had a lot to learn about some of the weird things that went on in so-called normal society. I mentioned earlier that I hadn't heard of bestiality until I went to Training School, but soon after arrival at Bedford I had to deal with a man who went out equipped with sugar lumps and carrots to make amorous advances towards a pretty pony in a field at Clapham, Bedford.

I won't go into the details of the case, except to say that the offender might have got away with his devious sexual acts if it wasn't for the Tesco's free bus service passing by. It was a double-decker bus and when it pulled up at a bus stop, all of the lady shoppers on the top deck had a ringside view of the performance on the other side of the hedge. Their accounts of the incident were quite animated!

The man was subsequently arrested and had a previous history of similar offences, so spent some time in Bedford prison.

On the evening shift when we weren't busy with specific policewomen's work and the Woman Sergeant had gone off duty, we were required to report to the male section Sergeant, who would allocate us work or a foot patrol. I had only been there a week when one of the male Sergeants asked me if I was a 'lesbian or a goer'. When I said "Pardon?" he said "You know – a bike or a dyke, all policewomen are one or the other and the men didn't want to waste their time with the wrong ones!" I replied "I'm not sure that I want to be either, so you will have to keep guessing". He then said, "You have been given number four as your collar number. The last number four was a goer, so you will have to take her place". This particular Sergeant was in his thirties, good looking and did have a certain arrogant charm, but I had already been warned that he was a married man, lecherous and liked to talk about his conquests in the canteen. Whether or not I was a 'goer', he was certainly a no go area, so I just laughed at him and walked away to get on with my duties. His behaviour may have encouraged the younger lads to try it on with the policewomen. Conversations were often peppered with innuendoes and chat up lines, but most of the girls used to simply play them at their own game. Any discomfort was disguised with laughter, as it certainly was not the done thing to show any weakness or embarrassment.

Sexual harassment and sexual discrimination was rife throughout the police service and Bedfordshire Police was no exception, but it wasn't recognised as such and simply reflected the norms of society at that time. As I knew no different, I learned to enjoy the attention and teasing, because at least it made me feel part of the group. I soon learned a few cutting remarks as 'put-downs', which could be used to good effect in the canteen if a guy needed putting in his place. Generally speaking if a female officer could overcome the sexist banter, demonstrate strength of character, a sense of humour and professional ability, she was soon accepted and gained respect for being an efficient police officer. There is no doubt that female officers had to work a lot harder to be accepted as part of the team, but once that happened the men were usually fiercely protective.

We patrolled on our own in those days, so it was important to be able to communicate with the police station when necessary. The old style police boxes and pillars had been phased out and radios had been phased in. The first type of personal radios issued was 'Motorola', but they were in two parts, a transmitter and a receiver, each about the size and weight of a house-brick! After a few years they were replaced by 'Pye Pocketfones', which were much lighter and more convenient. They did, however, have a pop-up aerial, which could be a bit painful if pushed carelessly, as it could end up your nose!

There weren't always enough personal radios to go round and the section patrol officers would take precedence. When allocated a foot patrol, if we didn't have a radio we were given a list of telephone kiosks (TKs) that became our points, where we had to be at a given time to receive calls. I remember upsetting one of the male Sergeants, who then gave me a foot beat with TKs so far apart that I nearly had to run to get there. It was snowing and I was absolutely frozen as I sheltered in the icy cold phone box at each point, waiting to see if I received a call. I was left in silence and felt totally forgotten, especially as the streets seemed to be deserted. My police greatcoat seemed to weigh a ton and my hands in leather gloves were frozen. I was miserable, shivering and shed a few tears of frustration, but then continued on my beat until it was time to return to the police station. On reporting back to the Sergeant, I smiled and told him how much I had enjoyed the walk. There was no way that I was going to whinge or appear weak. This would remain the case throughout my career, so the ability to put on a brave face was just another part of acting the role.

Missing person enquiries took up a great deal of our time. Over five hundred a year went missing in the Bedford area and usually we eventually traced all of them. We were very much aware of the human suffering involved in each case and handled our enquiries in as sensitive a way as possible.

Reasons for going missing were numerous. More than a third of missing persons were juvenile absconders from children's homes and they were particularly vulnerable to sexual exploitation. Teenagers also ran away from home after arguments with their parents, after committing crime or to be with their first love. Vulnerable elderly people often absent-mindedly departed from their regular routine, causing anxiety to their families. Other adults disappeared after a domestic dispute or when suffering from depression. Often, frantic parents would report losing a toddler in a busy shopping area or even at the home address.

On receiving a report of a missing person the first course of action was usually to visit the home address, check out the missing person's bedroom and search the premises in case the person had left clues or was hidden or trapped there. Children were sometimes found asleep in the most unlikely of places, such as in a wardrobe, laundry basket, coal-bunker or unused freezer.

In most cases a missing person form was completed and a full description and photograph obtained. It always surprised me how many people could not describe a member of their family with details such as height, weight, hair and eye colour. Asking a man what his wife was wearing when he last saw her was also often a difficult question!

Once we got enquiries under way, most missing persons were found within the first forty-eight hours. If necessary we would seek authority to utilise search parties, dogs and divers to search woodland or water, but of course there's a massive cost involved, so the initial enquiries had to be thorough. We would spend hours on door-to-door enquiries and investigative phone calls to individuals and agencies.

When we traced a missing person, there was always a sense of great satisfaction at a job well done. We would interview the person to establish the reason for going missing and whether or not they had been the subject of crime or had committed any crime. Vulnerable young people had sometimes been physically or sexually abused and our work became a crime investigation.

If a girl under sixteen years admitted that she had sexual intercourse with a man over sixteen years, there would usually be an offence of unlawful sexual intercourse (USI) or even rape and this was taken very seriously in line with the social morals of the time. The parents would be informed, a statement would be taken and a medical examination carried out by a doctor. This usually included a pregnancy test.

The contraceptive pill had been introduced on the National Health Service in the UK in 1961, but in my experience, young girls rarely had access to it and most relied on the man to use a contraceptive. Family doctors usually prescribed the pill mainly to older women who already had children and didn't want any more. It seemed that promiscuity was on the increase in the 1960s and 1970s, but the government and doctors didn't want to be seen to be encouraging "free love". Sex education was virtually non-existent in many schools and policewomen dealt with many frightened, naive young girls, who would then have to cope with unwanted pregnancies. I didn't realise it at the time but as a policewoman I was part of society's moral enforcement team. Young girls were not always shown a great deal of sympathy for their predicament, with comments such as "You should have thought about that before you had sex, or ran off with your boyfriend!" Girls were either returned to their parents, or in some cases taken into care. Meanwhile the boyfriend would be formally cautioned for the offence of USI, or if an older man were involved, a prosecution would follow.

The attitude of society started to change in 1974, when family planning clinics were authorised to prescribe the pill to single women. This was a controversial decision at the time, but certainly meant that young women had access to information on contraception. This also coincided with changes in the Policewomen's Departments, which I will describe in detail later, but meant that missing persons who were traced, were usually no longer subjected to in-depth interviews by policewomen, and offences of USI would usually be undetected. Pre-marital sexual relations were becoming the norm and more accepted by society.

After being traced, a missing person would usually be reunited with their loved ones, unless being an adult, they wanted their whereabouts kept secret. Juveniles had to be returned to a parent or taken into care, but if over seventeen years old and not wanting their whereabouts known, we would simply advise the parents that they were traced and alive and well. We certainly dealt with a lot of heartbreak.

As a young constable, I dreaded having to deliver sudden death messages to the next of kin. Generally speaking, members of the public fear something bad has happened, when a police officer knocks on their door. At training school, we had been taught to contact a neighbour or, where possible, find another family member to provide the required aftercare and support.

My first sympathetic message was to tell an elderly lady that her husband had died in hospital after routine surgery. I had been just about to return to the police station for my refreshment break, but diverted and drove an unmarked police car to the given address. It was in a row of cottages in High Street, Kempston.

I called in on the radio and asked if there were any other members of the family, but the answer was negative, so I thought that I would start by contacting a neighbour. My heart sank when I saw that all the other cottages were either empty or derelict. I then knocked on the lady's door wearing a serious, sad expression. I was greeted with a lovely smile. The lady seemed pleased to have a visitor and invited me in. Once we were sitting down I gave her the sad news and waited for a response. I expected her to be shocked and start to cry or at least be angry, but her response took me by surprise. She looked sad, but calmly said "Oh, it was Jack's birthday today. Just a minute!" She stood up, went over to a cupboard and got out a carefully wrapped present. She opened it revealing a bottle of Scotch and said, "Jack would have wanted us to have a little drop of this". I explained that I was on duty, so couldn't drink, but would stay and have a coffee with her while she had a little tipple. She insisted on making the coffee, which she made strong and black. We toasted her husband and as I started drinking I realised that she must have put a little drop of whisky in my coffee but drank it anyway. After half an hour, I got up to leave, but was decidedly a bit wobbly. I realised that I'd had a very generous tot of whiskey and no food, so the alcohol had gone straight to my head. The dear lady was smiling sweetly and thanked me for spending time with her. I knew that I would never live it down if I radioed the police station and admitted what had happened, so got into my police car and drove it very carefully back to the station yard. I breathed a sigh of relief when the car was safely parked and I made sure that I was sucking a mint when I went into the station to book off duty.

On another occasion I went to tell an elderly couple that their forty-five year old son, Albert, had died suddenly. They lived in a remote area and didn't have a telephone, so had no idea that he had been ill. When I arrived, I spoke to the wife and told her the sad news. Her husband had been asleep upstairs, so she woke him and asked him to come downstairs. Before he arrived, she asked me if I would tell him the news and I agreed. She then added "He's very deaf though, so you'll have to shout". I tried to be sensitive by just raising my voice but, after a few attempts, I found myself almost shouting "Albert's dead!" and eventually got the message through.

I realised that training simply cannot prepare you for every situation and it's not always easy to go by the book.

Domestic disputes were a regular part of our work. If a patrol officer was called to a domestic situation he would try to take a WPC with him. Domestics occurred in all walks of society, but came to our notice most often in blocks of flats or council estates where there was a close proximity of neighbours, who would phone the police on hearing screaming, banging or breaking glass.

Crimes of passion often led to actual or grievous bodily harm, arson or damage to property and such offences were often difficult to deal with. Aggression wasn't always just coming from the man and men were usually easier to cope with than hysterical women. The police role was to try to calm the situation and restore order. Sometimes, temporarily separating the couple was necessary. If an assault had occurred, the offender would be arrested and taken to Greyfriars Police Station. Often, the injured party would then refuse to make a statement of complaint and I've even been attacked by women, for taking their husbands away! Domestics could be very frustrating work and we would be called to the same house many times. We would use other agencies to offer support, but a court case was sometimes inevitable. I soon learned that it was not for police to judge the state of a relationship.

On one occasion, I was called to a house where a neighbour reported not seeing an elderly woman for some days and was concerned for the welfare of the lady and her husband. I knocked and the door was opened by the husband. I asked if his wife was well and was invited into the sitting room. The lady in question was lying on the floor near the fireplace and did not respond when I spoke to her. Her husband told me that she would sometimes curl up on the mat near the fire when she was feeling cold or sleepy. I knelt down by the lady and checked her vital signs. There was no pulse and rigour mortis had set in. I noted that there were no signs of injury. The husband seemed oblivious to her death and when asked when he last spoke to her, he said that he couldn't remember as they didn't talk to each other much these days. She hadn't eaten her dinner the previous evening and that morning he had stepped over his wife to get to kitchen. He had made a cup of tea, placed it on the hearth and wondered why she didn't bother to drink it! A post mortem later showed that the lady had died of natural causes, but that's what I call a sad relationship!

All Probationer Constables attended at least one post-mortem as part of their training. I suppose the logic was that once you have seen a body cut open you would be less shocked when you came across a dead body or a seriously injured person. Post-mortems are held when there is an unexplained cause of death and are usually followed by a Coroner's Inquest.

I attended my first post-mortem with two male probationer officers, under the supervision of a male Sergeant. I had been dreading the experience and hoped that I would deal with it in a professional way and without feeling ill. We were taken to the mortuary, which was next to Bedford Hospital and then the mortuary attendant brought in the corpse, which was the body of a young man in his thirties. The body was naked and the Sergeant, who was probably trying to lighten the atmosphere, made a joke about him being a well-hung young man. I found the remark very distasteful as I couldn't help but think that this was someone's son, brother or lover and even when dead, he deserved some respect. I realised that I had to cut out all thoughts of this being a human being and just concentrate on the clinical side of the process. The pathologist came in, introduced himself, and then got on with his work, using a selection of instruments. There is a pervading smell in a mortuary, which I had been warned about, so I was sucking an extra strong mint to mask the smell and it certainly helped, particularly when the first incision was made in the abdomen. One of the PCs felt faint and had to go outside, but I decided to detach my emotions and concentrate on the scientific process, which was very interesting and necessary for my learning. Organs were removed from the body, inspected, weighed and then preserved. Finally, the body was repacked and stitched up. The mortuary attendant was already tucking into his sandwiches by the time we left the mortuary!

I was relieved that the experience was over, but sadly it would not be the last that I would have to attend during my police service. I found that I was able to deal with it, because I knew that any pain and suffering for the individual was now over. It was when I attended the inquests, however, that my emotions sometimes got the better of me. The sight of grieving relatives reminded me that I might act tough when it came to the physical side of police work, but I still felt empathy and there was a vulnerable side to my character. Perhaps male and female officers felt the same, but emotions were never discussed back at the police station and any debrief would consist of a few drinks up at the bar and humorous stories about officers who had fainted at post-mortems.

When not engaged in their specialist duties, policewomen had their own foot beat area that covered the parks and riverside area. It always seemed like a real treat to be able to go out on foot patrol, particularly on a nice summer's day. Depending on the weather, the duty Sergeant would designate the dress standard for the day, either full uniform or shirt-sleeve order. Hats were always worn on outside duty, no matter what the weather, and woe betide any officer who was seen by a supervisor to be improperly dressed. If on foot beat and approached by an Inspector or other senior rank in uniform, we were required to salute them and they would return the salute. Sometimes, they would then ask to see your pocket book, check that all notes were up to date and sign the entry.

My favourite area on foot beat in Bedford covered the High Street and the lovely Embankment area alongside the River Ouse. There was always something happening there, especially on sunny days when the area was full of families and in the evenings when the pubs turned out. The river looked very beautiful, especially at night when it was illuminated with coloured lights, but unfortunately frequently seemed to attract drunken youths spilling over from the High Street. Occasionally bravado got the better of them and they would try to swim across the river and get caught by the currents. Then police would end up trying to rescue them or searching for a body.

One Sunday morning I was on patrol along the Embankment, when a young lad who was fishing saw a body in the reeds. I attended the scene and established that it was a man's body, so notified the control room by radio. They called out the diving team to recover the body, but there would be an hour's delay before they got to the scene. I was told by the controller to wait at the scene and try to keep the body out of public view until a screen could be erected. Unfortunately, once the bloated body had been disturbed, it kept floating to the surface and was not a pretty sight. I was aware that families were beginning to arrive in the area with young children, so every ten minutes or so, I leaned out and gently put my foot on the body and submerged it again. Maybe not a very dignified way to treat a body, but it was effective and I was just following orders to keep it out of public view.

Generally speaking though, foot patrol duty was fairly routine and a lot of the time was spent checking that premises were secure, stopping to chat to members of the public or dealing with simple road traffic offences.

The leafy lanes, parks and riverside paths drew families and young couples to the area, but also tended to attract some less desirable elements. We dealt with thefts, assaults, domestic arguments, missing persons and numerous local enquiries.

One day I received a complaint regarding a naked couple making love on the river bank in view of passers-by. The couple had been drinking and wouldn't listen to advice, so were arrested and taken to Greyfriars Police Station to cool down. Two hours later the Custody Sergeant cautioned and released the youngsters and within half an hour, another policewoman found them at it again in the park. Now that's what I call determination!

Policewomen were required to carry out plain clothes observations following complaints of indecent exposure or other sexual offences. Wearing civilian clothes and equipped with a radio, we took our turn strolling along the riverside paths or through the park trying to look relaxed, but just waiting to see if the offender would pick on us. It felt good to be able to make an arrest and turn the tables on men who were trying to shock or frighten women. We didn't seem to worry about the dangers involved in this work and regarded it as just part of the job.

Although we dealt with a range of serious and sometimes harrowing offences, there was no formal debriefing or counselling for policewomen, but the policewomen's department did offer a supportive environment. The Women Sergeants certainly kept an eye on their young policewomen and when we were left unsupervised, we would share our experiences and often see the funny side of dire circumstances. Also within the police station environment, there was lots of support and good-natured humour from our male colleagues. They may have teased their female colleagues and sometimes stepped over the mark with sexist comments, but generally speaking, we were valued members of staff and very happy in our work.

After completing nearly two years as a Probationer Constable, I attended a two-week Continuation Training course at Bruche, near Warrington. Bruche was the training centre for the North-West region of the UK, but I had been sent there as it accepted women officers. There were seventeen constables on the course, with only two females. I sounded like a lone voice amongst all the northern accents, but soon felt very much part of the group. The police service is like a big family, welcoming 'distant cousins' and wherever police officers get together, there is a shared culture and sense of humour.

Unlike initial training, I felt that we were treated more as responsible adults and I enjoyed the experience. On the other hand, I had gained in confidence and was able to 'hold my own' in any situation. At the end of the Continuation Course I returned to my Force ready for new challenges. Having successfully completed Probationer Training, I was now a fully-fledged police officer and would be seeking opportunities to enhance my career.

At my annual appraisal, I expressed an interest in work in the Criminal Investigation Department (CID). I hoped that I would have the opportunity of an 'Aide to CID' attachment. This was rather like an apprenticeship and successful completion would enhance my chance of future selection. Sometimes in life, it's important to get noticed and stand out from the crowd.

As luck would have it, I got my opportunity. I was on patrol in Bedford, driving the unmarked policewomen's car, when a message came over the car radio. There had been an armed robbery at a betting shop in the London area. Four male suspects had left the scene in an old London taxi, which it was believed was heading north on the M1. A part registration number was given and any sightings were to be reported.

Five minutes later I saw a vehicle answering the description, travelling along Midland Road, Bedford, towards the railway station. I radioed control and was instructed to tail the vehicle until back-up arrived. The taxi then suddenly swerved into the railway station car park and ended up at an angle near the fence. I saw that the position stopped two of the men from being able to get out of the nearside doors, but the driver's door was partly opened. I radioed in to say that suspects were decamping and then pulled my car across the rear offside passenger door. I jumped out and grabbed the driver who was attempting to get out. He was as drunk as a skunk, as were the others in the car and I met very little resistance. I'm not sure they realised what was happening, but I soon had back up and all four men were arrested. To be honest, this was one of the easiest arrests I had ever made. The circumstances were totally bizarre and the Met Police came and took away the prisoners, but I got a commendation. I was simply in the right place at the right time, but it got me noticed by the hierarchy.

Chapter 4

Sex for Sale

Bedford in 1970, in common with many other large cosmopolitan towns, occasionally experienced problems with prostitution, mainly centred in the town centre area. In Bedford, the problem surfaced in Midland Road, an area adjacent to the railway station, and in Tavistock Street, an area which attracted late night punters because of its wealth of fast food and Indian and Chinese restaurants. Prostitution is not unlawful, but soliciting for trade in a public place or running a brothel is, and these offences usually only came to light when a member of the public made a complaint.

As a woman police officer, my duties at the time included the investigation and detection of offences involving sexual offences, vice and prostitution. Acquiring expertise in these areas was often by way of experience, trial and error and I acknowledged that, with my fairly sheltered upbringing, I had lots to learn.

At Police Training School, I had learned the law concerning sexual offences and my Woman Sergeants had advised me on the local procedures concerning the cautioning of prostitutes. This involved observing females approaching male clients in the street or public place and touting for business. The male clients often cruised the area in cars, while they checked out the 'goods' on offer. The working girls would stand at the kerb either talking to the men in vehicles or stopping them as they walked along the pavement. On witnessing this behaviour on a first occasion, the prostitute would be approached by the police officer. The prospective client usually then disappeared rapidly in a cloud of exhaust fumes. The prostitute's details were then taken (whatever name she chose to give) and she would be advised regarding her conduct of soliciting in a public place. The police officer was then usually treated to a few colourful words of advice from the prostitute. Personally, I never fancied doing that with my truncheon! These exchanges were really quite harmless and all part of the initiation for a young policewoman.

On returning to the police station, the policewoman would make an entry in the Street Offences Register about the advice given. Then, if the same prostitute was observed on a subsequent occasion, she would be arrested and taken to the police station. A further entry was made in the Street Offences Register. This register was a hefty leather bound tome, seemingly originating from time immemorial and it certainly contained a few details of immoral goings on that were generally hidden from the public eye. Having been caught twice acting in an immoral way, the prostitute would be formally cautioned by the Duty Inspector, offered welfare advice and again released to entertain her public. If she was subsequently caught again, she would appear before the court as a common prostitute.

As a young officer, wishing to prove my ability in applying the law, I dutifully applied my learning and subsequently cautioned and arrested several prostitutes. Somehow, the size of the Street Offences Register and the fact that all entries were to be made using a fountain pen seemed to add weight to the nature of the offence. Like all female probationer constables, it was also regarded as essential that I receive a tick in my Probationer Record book against the heading 'prostitute dealt with'.

In many ways, however, the experience was rather an anti-climax (for me, although one hopes not for the clients!) because prostitutes rarely measured up to my stereotype. Although some of the younger ones were attractive, sexy looking tarts with heavy make-up, skimpy clothing and thigh length boots, many of our 'ladies of the night' were very ordinary, fairly dowdy looking women dressed in cheap clothing, trying to make a few extra bob to make ends meet for the family. The biggest causes for concern were vulnerable young girls who had been enticed into this line of work by men who befriended them as boyfriends and then acted as pimps and lived on the immoral earnings. These girls had sometimes grown up in local authority care and were well known to the police as frequent missing persons. We did our best to deter them from prostitution and provide contacts for ongoing support, but I was not convinced that receiving moral advice from a 'rookie cop' was going to change their way of life. On the other hand, I learned a great deal from my conversations with prostitutes and my knowledge of fetishes, fantasies and financial deals was greatly enhanced!

A learning experience arose for me following a complaint from a shopkeeper in Midland Road, Bedford. Apparently, prostitutes were plying for trade outside his shop and upsetting some of his customers. He believed that several taxi drivers were also involved in conveying the girls and their clients to local brothels. Initial observations were carried out by plain-clothed male officers. They confirmed that there was some evidence to support the allegations. A policewoman was now required to carry out plain clothes observations and patrol Midland Road, alongside the other working girls. I entered wholeheartedly into the role, letting down my shoulder length hair from the regulation bun net, applying bright red lipstick, and wearing a tight black jumper, purple mini skirt and high heeled purple suede boots. As a twenty-three year old single woman, I had been given the perfect excuse to temporarily discard my usual rather severe police uniform and dress in a sexy manner. I loved all the attention I was getting from my male colleagues. I was duly dispatched to walk the patch in Midland Road and was told not to worry as a Woman Sergeant and a male constable would be observing me from a nearby vehicle. If I went off on foot or in a vehicle then they would follow me. I was to speak to other prostitutes, pimps, clients, taxi drivers or anyone who showed an interest. The object was to play it cool and obtain as much information as possible concerning the regular procedures in Midland Road. There was no CCTV in those days so I was to be eyes and ears out on the street and if necessary act as a newcomer to the game.

It was about 10 p.m. and dark apart from the street lights and neon signs in Midland Road with its selection of pubs, restaurants, chip shops, dance halls and snooker clubs. Although I had walked this beat confidently on many occasions in my police uniform, I now felt very different in my new role. I felt vulnerable, but excited as I teetered along in my high-heeled boots, eyeing up potential punters, but not making any obvious moves. I was aware of a row of parked cars about thirty yards away and guessed that my colleagues would be observing from this vantage-point. I had also become aware of other girls in the area, some of whom gave me watchful looks, but after about twenty minutes I was beginning to get rather bored and perhaps slightly offended that I had not been approached and propositioned. My colleagues would think that, even dressed like this, I couldn't pull a man and I could imagine the chat in the canteen. Surely some gorgeous hunk on a night out would come and chat me up before long? Then, just as I was about to cross over to the other side of the road, and stood at the edge of the kerb, I heard someone say, 'I like you. You do 'jigger jig'? How much? I turned to face the speaker, but found myself looking straight over his head. I am five feet, seven inches tall and was wearing three inch high heels and he was only about five feet, two inches. He was of Asian origin and his English was not fluent, but he looked me up and down in a lecherous way and made himself quite clear. He repeated, 'I like jigger jig. How much?" I started to forget my brief and attempted to tell him to push off, when suddenly he put his arm around me, tried to grope my breast and said "'I love you. Jigger jig for a pound!" The indignity and humiliation of a £1 offer was too much for me. I swung at him with my right hand and smacked him so hard that he reeled back across the pavement. He steadied himself and then hurried off down a side street. Before I had chance to do anything my Sergeant and PC colleagues were standing next to me. The Sergeant asked what happened, but failed to see the funny side of it and told me quite sternly that I had blown it as I was not supposed to hit the punters. In contrast, the look on the PC's face suggested that he was stifling a laugh just long enough to reach the station canteen. Upon my return to the station, the tea fund tin was rattled in my direction and loose change was offered by several of the station wags. I smiled and joined in the fun, but was also determined to establish what the going rate was in Midland Road. I needed to know where I had gone wrong.

My opportunity for further research came after there had been a murder in town. The female victim was believed to be a prostitute and I was one of the team of plain-clothes policewomen who were to visit some of the lower class pubs in Bedford and chat to the prostitutes. The girls were given cards and invited to make contact with local police if they had any information. We spent a few weeks on this task; information was forthcoming and the detectives got their man.

As an added bonus for me, during the course of enquiries, I got to know several of the prostitutes on a friendly, chatty basis and they shared a few of their trade secrets. I asked several of the girls what the going rate was along Midland Road. There was agreement that for basic sex with immigrant workers the rate was £1 for 'satisfaction' (Equivalent to £12 in 2015). I showed surprise, so one of the girls explained that immigrant workers often lived six to a bedroom, sometimes even more at shift changeover times. If the performance with the first client was good enough while the others stood waiting, satisfaction came all too quickly for some and the girl picked up a minimum of £6. The girls laughed about this 'jigger jig' special offer, male frailty and generally enjoyed furthering my education. I was fascinated with their candid reality, their humour, but also with the sense of dignity of one woman who said," At least I feed and clothe my own kids and don't have to rely on charity". Another prostitute asked me to consider if there really was a difference between what they did and the way in which rich women gave sexual favours for posh flats, nice restaurant meals or expensive jewellery. Her final comment was that £1 can seem a great deal at the end of the week when there is nothing for the kids' tea.

Regardless of the sordid background, It was difficult not to like these women and in learning about their own brand of dignity, I had recovered a little of my own.

My education was also furthered when I had occasion to visit a brothel or the home of a working girl. Sometimes these visits occurred after one of the girls had been arrested for shoplifting and we went to search their home for further stolen goods. On occasions, we found more than we bargained for, as we uncovered sex toys and equipment used in a variety of erotic practices, involving dominance and submission.

I sometimes also accompanied a male Sergeant when he carried out his routine visits to licensed premises, which included the sex shop. These may have been common in the big cities, but I think we only had one in Tavistock Street,

Bedford and this was fairly new on the scene. I remember reading an article in the local newspaper, where residents expressed their dismay and disgust that such a place existed in their locality. On entering the shop, the Sergeant spoke to the manager and then we wandered around the shop checking out the contents, especially the pornographic videos. If any of them appeared to be unlawful pornography, which usually meant sex involving animals or children, we would seize the items for further investigation. That meant going back to the police station and finding a quiet place to view the videos, making notes and then, if necessary, preparing a report to submit to the Director of Public Prosecutions (DPP). Most of the items I viewed had salacious titles to encourage sales and although the content was dubious, it was deemed to be within the law. Prior to this, I had never seen a pornographic video, so it was a steep learning curve and an experience only to be shared with the most trusted of colleagues, although the number of volunteers was endless!

Chapter 5

Secret Assignment

It was a surprise and somewhat intriguing to be summoned to attend the office of the Detective Chief Superintendent (DCS) at Police Headquarters. In those days, constables only attended the hallowed offices of Police HQ for hiring, firing, a discipline hearing, commendation, or the award of a medal. Since I didn't think I qualified for any of them, I was feeling rather anxious as I walked, in full uniform, towards HQ. I reported to the receptionist and was required to take a seat in the rather grand reception hall. The 'Pines' was a large Victorian house with a polished, open wooden, balustraded staircase, leading to its many floors. This building was known to most of Bedfordshire Police staff as the 'Ivory Towers', as it and its staff seemed so remote from the rest of the Force.

I had met, or at least seen and heard the Detective Chief Superintendent (DCS), during several of his visits to Greyfriars Police Station, usually at the time of a major enquiry. He was a thick-set man, with black hair, thick black eyebrows, which gave his dark eyes a hooded appearance. He always wore dark, expensive looking suits and well-polished shoes. His overall dark looks seemed to match his temper. I had heard him raise his voice angrily on a number of occasions and had been grateful that his expletives were not directed at me. Perhaps my luck had now run out.

After what seemed like an interminable wait, the receptionist told me that I was to go upstairs, as the DCS was ready to see me. I walked up several flights of stairs, reached his office marked by a name plaque on the door. On the doorpost was mounted a light system resembling traffic lights. I knocked on the door and a green traffic light was illuminated saying 'Enter'. On doing so, I was confronted by the DCS, who was sitting behind an enormous executive style desk. I was wearing my uniform hat and as this was a senior officer, I came to attention and delivered a smart salute. I later found out that the DCS neither expected nor appreciated salutes.

He indicated that I should sit on the chair, strategically placed in front of the desk. To my surprise, he then spoke to me in a friendly, rather gentle manner, reassuring me that I had not done anything wrong, but had been selected for a special task.

He told me that he thought I was a bright, intelligent young woman, who was showing potential for a future in CID and wanted to give me a special opportunity to show my initiative. Bedfordshire Police had been selected to assist a national agency in running an exercise of special importance. The job was top secret and I would be required to sign the Official Secrets Act. I would then be working for Special Branch (SB) and would be given information on a need to know basis, but at some stage, I would be required to go to a pub and make the acquaintance of a man.

I was naive and suitably flattered to have been specially selected, so agreed to accept the assignment. I was told to clear any urgent paperwork and then go on special leave until I received further instructions

I asked the DCS if my divisional senior officers and supervisors knew about the assignment, or if I was to inform them. He advised me that they knew I was doing a job for him and would be on special leave. I was given a clear instruction not to discuss my brief with anyone else, including my colleagues, family and friends.

He then made it clear that our conversation was at an end and that any future contact would be with the Detective Chief Inspector (DCI), who then showed me from the office and arranged contact times.

As I walked down the main staircase to reception, I felt slightly light-headed. I was relieved that I was not in trouble and flattered that I had been selected for an important assignment, the secret nature of which made it rather intriguing and exciting. In any case, it would make a change from dealing with sexual offences and missing persons or walking the beat.

On returning to Greyfriars Police Station, it was obvious that my supervisors had been told not to ask questions and accepted that I would be absent for a while. I cleared my desk and prepared to go on leave.

Before I left, I had a meeting with a member of SB, who showed me a photograph of the young man that I would be expected to meet. He was in his late twenties and reasonably attractive with short auburn coloured hair. The only requirement during leave was that I was to telephone the DCI daily at specified times and follow his instructions. I was otherwise free to enjoy my extra time off.

After a few days, I was instructed to hire a car of my choice for the following day. I had been given an initial sum of cash and advised that all additional expenses would be reimbursed. I made the necessary hire arrangements and then sorted out my clothes for the following day. I chose a figure hugging slinky top, a black mini skirt, leather jacket and high-heeled knee length suede boots. My shoulder length black hair was worn in a loose style and my makeup and jewellery were carefully chosen, so I was feeling quite pleased with myself. I had been advised by the DCI that I would receive specific instructions the next day, but to be prepared that the 'exercise' could last more than one day. I was single, lived in my own flat and had no pets, so that did not pose a problem. After making my last minute preparations, I went to bed, but hardy slept a wink owing to the excitement and uncertainty of the day to come.

The following morning I made telephone contact with the DCI and was given my final instructions. I was told to make sure that the car I hired was an estate car, big enough to put a bicycle in if necessary. I found this amusing, as it hardly sounded like a romantic date was in store for me. I was given the location of a pub in a rural village in the north of Bedfordshire, where I was to meet the man whose photo I had been shown. I was given a specific time to arrive and told that I was to use my initiative to get this man to accept a lift in my car. Apparently, I would be under police surveillance during the time at the pub. When I left, I would be followed and may be stopped by police officers. At no time was I to reveal that I was a police officer and my colleagues would have been briefed not to show any sign of recognition. The rest of the scenario would be played according to outcomes.

As directed, I drove to the pub location at 7 pm. I had hired a large estate vehicle, but there was no difficulty in parking as the car park was nearly empty, suggesting that most other customers would be locals from the village. I had been advised that my contact may arrive on a bicycle, but there was none to be seen in the car park. Just as I was about to enter the front door of the pub, I saw my contact arrive and alight from his bike. He was very casually and boringly dressed in sweater and trousers and his outfit was completed by cycle clips! His hair in the photo had been a subtle auburn colour neatly styled, but this man had a shock of ginger hair that looked wild and windswept. The idea that I was to pick up this man by 'any means' suddenly seemed quite ridiculous, as he certainly bore no resemblance to my ideal date. I recalled the words of the DCI that the man I met would be 'a good looking, very fit young man' whom a young woman like me would find 'most attractive'. Some areas of his research were clearly lacking!

The more I thought about it, the more I became aware of the bizarre nature of the task that I had taken on. What if I couldn't get the man to come with me? What was I supposed to do to keep him with me until someone intervened? The briefing had not covered these finer points and it seemed that I was supposed to use my initiative. Anyway, there was now a job to be done and it was too late for me to change my mind, so I walked into the pub. There was a warm friendly atmosphere with half a dozen locals sitting around the bar chatting amicably with the barman, but as soon as I entered, all conversation stopped. They all turned to look me up and down. Most of them looked as though they had just come from work on the farms. I suddenly felt very uneasy, overdressed and wondered if they thought I was 'a tart on the pull'. I didn't usually go into pubs on my own, so this was a new and rather embarrassing scenario for me. I just reminded myself that I had a job to do and went up to the bar, smiled at everyone and ordered myself a glass of wine. I sat at a table between the door and the bar, with my back to the wall so that I could see all comings and goings.

After a few minutes, my contact, who I had been told was called Steve, walked into the pub and over to the bar. He looked slightly better now that he had removed his cycle clips and tidied his hair. He had a pleasant face and a good physique. He ordered a beer in a well-cultured, manly voice and then without giving me so much as a glance, he walked to the far end of the bar. He sat at a table about fifteen yards from where I was sitting. He had his back to the wall and was facing the front door, but he promptly pulled a newspaper from his pocket and started to read, so that he was hidden from view. I felt that I would have more luck with the guys at the bar rather than with him. I also surreptitiously looked around for any plain-clothes police officer, who would, as promised, have me under surveillance, but there were no likely candidates in the pub. The farmer types seemed unlikely, so maybe I was on my own after all, unless of course there was a hidden camera. This was clearly not something that the DCI felt I needed to know, but I felt sure that he had it covered. I put my mind on my job and started to think of tactics to get close to my contact and eventually engage him in conversation.

After about twenty minutes, I noticed that Steve had looked around the bar, checked his watch and then went back to reading his paper. I got up, ordered myself another drink and asked for change for the fruit machine, which was down at the far end of the bar where Steve was sitting. I casually mentioned to the barman that I was waiting for my boyfriend, who had obviously been delayed. I then went to play on the fruit machine, so that I was standing only a few yards from Steve. As this was on expenses, I fed the fruit machine about £5 in coins, which to me seemed a great extravagance. I did not even get so much as a glance from Steve, who remained behind his newspaper. I then sat down at a nearby table, took my chequebook from my handbag, under the pretext of writing a cheque. I stood up and went over to Steve and said 'Excuse me. Do you have a pen that I could borrow for a few minutes?' With only half a glance he took a pen from his pocket, handed it to me and immediately returned behind his paper. I thanked him and sat down. About ten minutes later I noticed Steve again look at his watch; fold his newspaper and then stand up to leave. I then thanked him for the loan of the pen and said, "Have you been stood up as well? My boyfriend was supposed to meet me here when he finished work in Northampton. I don't know what's happened but he's not turned up." Steve confirmed that he was also supposed to meet someone. I told him that I was a librarian and that it had been a long day, so I would be going home soon. I commented that the pub was in a remote location and it was just starting to rain so wondered if I could offer him a lift. He said that he regretted that this would not be possible as he had a bicycle with him and was stuck with having to cycle all the way to Bedford. Of course, I then told him that (by amazing coincidence!) I had an estate car and could probably fit his bike in the back if that would be of any assistance. This was all too corny to be true, so I was amazed when he gratefully accepted my offer of a lift. I said "Good night" to the barman and told him that if my boyfriend came in, would he please tell him that I had gone home.

Having stowed the bicycle in the car and Steve in the passenger seat, I set off to drive to Bedford about eight miles away. It was dark, but the A6 road was fairly well lit and very quiet. Steve and I made general conversation. As we neared Clapham on the outskirts of Bedford, a police traffic car suddenly came from behind and then overtook us, before putting on his 'Stop' sign. Another marked police patrol car pulled behind us as I slowed and eventually stopped. I said to Steve, "What the bloody hell do this lot want?" and within seconds my driver's door was pulled open and I was shouted at to get out of the vehicle and put my hands on the bonnet. I expressed my indignation with a few swear words thrown in. The police officers then searched my car and to my genuine surprise found a plastic bag containing white powder under the passenger seat. They then adopted an aggressive attitude towards me and I did not find it difficult to respond with aggression and indignation. They commented that they knew about my history of being a drug pusher. By this time, Steve was also standing with his hands on the roof of the car, while being frisked by one of the officers. I told them that Steve had nothing to do with it. I had just met him in a pub and was giving him a lift to Bedford. Needless to say, this did not convince the officers, who arrested us both on suspicion of being in possession of Class A drugs. We were handcuffed, put into separate cars and taken to Greyfriars Police Station.

On arrival in the back yard of the police station and within hearing of Steve, I loudly protested my innocence and told those 'bastard coppers' to take their hands off me. I'd had plenty of experience of stroppy prisoners and was quite enjoying my acting role. I was then pushed towards the door of the charge room where the custody officer waited to receive his prisoners. There was, as directed, no sign of recognition on either of our parts. Routine details were taken and a charge sheet completed for both Steve and me. I was using my true name, address and date of birth. Both our names were entered in the Station arrest register. We had both been arrested on suspicion of possessing a controlled drug, but my sheet also showed that I was suspected of supplying drugs to others. I protested my innocence and demanded a phone call, but was told to shut up and wait. I noticed a few of my police colleagues taking a glance through the observation window situated in the enquiry office area. I hoped that they knew that this was an exercise, as suddenly it all seemed a bit too real for comfort. I could just imagine the gossip around the station and knew that I would soon find out who my true friends were. The Custody Sergeant acted in a very cool professional manner as he directed his staff to take the prisoners to the cells.

The male and female cells at Greyfriars Police Station were located in separate corridors, with an adjoining corridor and exercise yard between them. I knew from previous custody experience that voices from one cellblock were just audible to prisoners in the other, so I knew that the action of placing me in a cell had a purpose in the exercise. Nonetheless, as my escort silently walked me to my cell, I began to feel very uneasy. He was after all a colleague, but there were no whispered words of comfort or understanding.

As the heavy steel cell door was banged behind me, I began to feel totally isolated. Like all cells, mine had a wooden bunk style bed against the wall, with two grimy grey coloured blankets on top of it. The only light source was from a small ceiling light covered by a metal cage and controlled by the gaoler from outside the cell. During the day there would be light from a small block glass window situated high on the wall adjacent to the exercise yard. There were no toilets or sinks in the cells, so there was a bell to be pushed if a prisoner needed to use a toilet. Sometimes prisoners, particularly drunks, just used the cell floor, so regardless of a daily mop with strong disinfectant the cellblocks still smelled very unpleasant, rather like a public toilet. I had always detested gaoler duty in the female cells, but it was now far worse on the inside and I hoped that the exercise would soon be over.

I kept expecting to see the DCI and was relieved when I heard footsteps approaching my cell, but it was a policewoman who came in. She said, "I've been told to carry out a strip search for drugs". I had been happy to roleplay the part of a prisoner, but there was no way that I was going to suffer the humiliation of being strip-searched by a colleague. I told her that if she tried to do so I would fight her, so the only way out of the situation was for her to pretend to have searched me and sign the record accordingly. She said that she had been told not to talk to me, but to treat me like a normal prisoner. My colleagues had all heard of my arrest and been shocked. They had not been told that it was an exercise. She decided to trust me, and left to sign the custody record to say that I had been searched with a negative result. I was then alone with my thoughts and felt decidedly uneasy. Some of my colleagues clearly believed that I had committed a crime and I felt that I had been foolish to keep the secret as directed. Apart from the DCS and DCI, nobody knew of my innocence. I had after all been found in a hire car with a quantity of drugs in my possession and accompanied by a stranger whom I had picked up in a pub. Even if I told anyone the truth, they would find it a most unlikely story! I began to wonder if there could possibly be an elaborate plan to set me up for some reason.

After I had been in the cell for over a few hours I received a visit from the DCI, who gestured that I should follow him to the Matron's Room, which was at the far end of the corridor. After closing the door, we had a conversation. He complimented me on doing a good job. I told him that I was beginning to feel very uneasy about the situation, as nobody else knew the truth about my arrest. The DCI then did his best to reassure me and agreed that I could spend the night in the relative comfort of the matron's room, as long as I returned to a cell early the next morning.

He also told me that I wasn't to worry, but should be aware that in the morning I might be charged with drug offences and appear before the court with Steve as my co-defendant. I expressed my disquiet, so to allay my fears, the DCI decided to tell me more about the exercise, which was run by Special Branch in conjunction with MI5. It was the final test for Steve, a trainee spy. He was now being interviewed by Special Branch and Drug Squad officers and would either break and tell them who he was or would face a court appearance and conviction for drug offences.

The following morning, I had the opportunity to wash and make myself comfortable before returning to my cell, where I ate my breakfast off a metal tray with a plastic spoon. I was then taken to the charge room, where I saw

Steve looking very pale and haggard. I felt truly sorry for him. He looked up and gave me a blank expression. We were both required to stand in front of the charge desk while we were formally charged with drug offences. I was handed a copy of the charge sheet and then returned to my cell.

I expected to go to Court that morning, but nothing happened. Then just before midday, the DCI came to my cell and told me that it was over. Steve had finally given them the information necessary to clear his name and in doing so, had failed his final test. I was taken to an interview room to see him. Steve stood as I went into the room and held out his hand. He gave me a wry smile and told me that I should have been an actress rather than a policewoman as I had played my part very convincingly. I told him that I felt very sorry to have brought about his downfall in the exercise, but he was very gallant and told me that I could have saved him from a much worse situation in real life.

I was then debriefed by a Special Branch officer who thanked me for doing an excellent job and said that a commendation would be recorded on my record, but would never get an official mention, as it was secret. I never did find out if he was serious or just having a laugh at my expense.

The following day I returned to normal duties. Most of my colleagues said that they had known that I was innocent, but I understand that there were a few who had some doubts! My part in this exercise was never mentioned again, but within six months, I was appointed to CID.

Chapter 6

Detective Days

In August 1971 I began a three-month 'Aide to CID'. This was a type of apprenticeship as a detective. Successful completion could lead to a future appointment as a detective, where one would work in plain clothes investigating and detecting a range of crimes. I had already worked with CID on a number of serious crimes and was keen to do well during my time as an aide, as I saw CID as a career path. There had not been a woman detective at Bedford for a number of years, since the retirement of Gwen Wooding. She was a very experienced, rather genteel policewoman of the old school, in her fifties, but seemed well able to deal with any man or villain who gave her any nonsense. She would be a difficult act to follow, especially for a woman in her twenties, so I knew that I would have to develop my own style and work very hard to gain credibility in CID.

I enjoyed the opportunity to wear civilian clothes rather than uniform and decided that my work outfits would be smart and fashionable. We did get a plain clothes allowance, so I bought two suits, one black and one white. Miniskirts were in fashion at the time and both suits had short skirts, but were more demure than the pelmets worn by many girls at that time. The outfits were complete with knee-length, white shiny stretch boots or purple suede boots, which were the height of fashion at that time. Instead of wearing my long, black hair in the usual regulation style bun, I was now able to wear it in the fashionable 1960's style, back-combed on top and flicked up around the shoulders. I also had great fun with a blonde wig, which was very useful when I was carrying out observations and didn't want to be recognised.

I now rather enjoyed going to work, looking and feeling feminine, whilst still demonstrating that I was very capable of doing a good job investigating crimes.

Whilst working as an aide, I worked with most of the detectives in CID, learning about different investigative styles and interview techniques. It seemed that I was a useful part of the team, especially when it came to carrying out plain clothes observations or using feminine charms to gain information. At the end of three months, I received a favourable report and hoped that I would be considered when a vacancy arose in the department. I returned to uniform duties, but before long as a result of undercover successes and good arrests for crime, I was selected for CID.

In March 1972, I attended a twelve-week CID course at the Home Office Detective Training School located at Mather Avenue, Liverpool.

We studied Criminal Law and the investigation of serious crime. Specialist lecturers taught us about murder investigations, the preservation of a crime scene, the bagging of evidence and the interviewing of suspects. We also had a session on pornography, which involved watching a number of films to establish the difference between legal and unlawful pornography. In a class of thirty, there were four women and we all stayed in the room, even though it was embarrassing to hear the crude comments from a few of our male colleagues.

In addition to our studies, there was also an opportunity to experience the delights of the city of Liverpool, much of which was a real eye-opener to a girl from the southern counties. The course directors explained to us that they could teach us criminal law and procedure, but it was the practical side of investigation that made good detectives. This included visiting a wide range of premises and dealing with a broad spectrum of society. We were going to be given the opportunity to visit many of Liverpool's clubs and see how the police worked their contacts. The four local detectives on our course each took a group out most evenings to visit a range of clubs. I don't remember them all but do recall the SHE Club which was very plush, but had some of the most attractive and expensive hookers in town. The Cabin Club which was more of a dive than I could have imagined and a West Indian shebeen (illicit drinking club), where illicit alcohol was freely available, but the music was amazing. I was the only white woman in the crowded and rather dark room, when a West Indian man came and asked me to dance. I got a nod from the guys and went out onto the dance floor. When asked my name, I said 'Samantha' and after one dance, the man held me tight and said "We'll go outside Samantha, have a bit of fun and maybe make a baby". Fortunately, my colleagues saw my frantic wave, so came and rescued me!

It was quite an experience doing the clubs, but it wasn't just for fun. It was acknowledged that for many of us it would be essential to get to know club owners and develop informants in this type of premises.

As a special treat, our course directors organised a visit to Anfield, the home of Liverpool Football Club and one of the most famous stadiums in the world. I knew nothing about football so didn't know what to expect when we were told that we would be in the Kop. I soon found out that it was an enormous terrace behind one of the goals at Anfield, capable of holding as many as twenty-seven thousand supporters. It had one hundred steps and towered above the Walton Breck Road, behind the ground. My male colleagues all loved the experience, but I hated it. We were right at the back and packed in like sardines and when the fans decided to sway in unison, there was no option but to go with the flow. The chanting and singing fans generated lots of noise that reverberated under the steel roof. Worst of all, it soon became obvious that going to the toilet was impossible, so male fans were peeing on the steps or down onto the road below. A fight started when one peed in the coat pocket of the man next to him! It was an experience, but one that I was glad never to repeat.

A CID evening out in Liverpool would often end up with drinks in one of the late night venues. On one such occasion I went with seven of the lads to a hotel, which had a licence extension owing to its live music, even though it consisted of an elderly pianist in the ballroom. As we entered, the pianist asked if I had a request and I asked him to play 'Elvis's Love Me Tender'. His rendition was awful, but I danced with a colleague and then went to sit down. The pianist said "You play a song for a lady and she doesn't even give you a clap" to which my colleague replied "You're lucky mate – she's given it to everyone else!"

I returned to Greyfriars Police Station, where I was accepted as part of CID, previously an all-male team. My colleagues included some very clever old style detectives, each with their own unique character and a devilish sense of humour. I had to work very hard to gain their acceptance. Fortunately, my Detective Sergeant was a real gentleman, who treated me with respect. He allocated me a wide range of jobs, which gave me a chance to prove myself.

CID officers at that time were a dedicated, hardworking team, but there was also a drinking culture, whereby everyone went to the pub, either individually to meet informants during the shift, or together with colleagues at the end of late shift. Initially, I tried to keep up with the men but after getting quite tipsy on a few occasions, I realised that I didn't have their capacity for drinking and smoking. I decided to stay in the office to get my reports done and then maybe join them for one drink. It was important for me to feel part of the team, but I had no intention of losing my femininity by drinking, swearing and trying to be one of the lads.

I'd only been in CID a week when four of my colleagues came back from the pub in high spirits. I was working in the office and one of them said "Isn't it time for the initiation?" and picked up the date stamp off the desk. I had heard a rumour about initiation procedures in CID offices across the country and there was no way that I was going to let them stamp my bare behind. I was terrified and backed into the corner and as they approached laughing. I said "OK if you mark me, I'll mark you. The first one to touch me will have a fight and get his face scratched!" The response was "Oh come on be a sport" but then they backed off and went home. I was shocked as these were my colleagues, but it did seem that I had won some respect that evening, as they never tried it again.

I became very much part of the team and accepted every job allocated to me with enthusiasm, because I knew that I had to prove my worth. Like our uniformed colleagues, we attended all sorts of homes and adapted our communication style to the occupants. I generally adopted a friendly approach, only reverting to an authoritarian approach when necessary. If offered a cup of tea it was usually advantageous to accept as it gave time to chat and gain information in an informal way. Sometimes though, the tea would be left, as I couldn't face drinking it once I had seen or smelled the unhygienic conditions in the house and especially the kitchen. One definite indicator was when I found my feet sticking to the carpet or linoleum owing to the ingrained filth. It was then also a good idea to choose to sit on a hard wooden chair rather than on the tacky soft furnishings of the settee or armchair. I was never offended by poverty, but was often disgusted by the filth that some people regarded as acceptable in their homes. I had been brought up in a relatively poor area of South Shields in Tyneside, but had been taught that cleanliness and good manners were important and cost very little. I found myself being very judgemental when I saw families living in squalor and children running wild while the parents drank, smoked and watched television.

It was the norm for CID officers to attend burglaries where high value goods had been stolen. On one occasion I received a report that expensive jewellery had been taken from a high-class home in Biddenham, which was the stock-broker and millionaire part of Bedford. I attended with a burly male detective to interview the lady of the house. We parked the police car on the driveway and knocked on the door, which was answered by the housekeeper. She, then called the lady of the house, who looked my colleague and I up and down and said "I suppose you'd better come in, but do take off your shoes!" We obliged and then walked across polished floors and pure cream carpet into a sitting room with cream carpet, cream curtains, and cream leather suite. I don't think I'd ever seen such a beautiful home before, but it looked more like a Hollywood film set than a lived-in home. The lady beckoned to us to take a seat, but on noting our dark suits, she suddenly lunged across the room and pushed large cushions under us. She then asked if we would like tea and arranged for the housekeeper to fetch it. I took a statement from the lady and asked her if she had photographs of the stolen items. While she was out the room, we relaxed and decided to enjoy the tea and biscuits, which were on the nearby coffee table. The tea had been poured into dainty china cups and the homemade shortbread biscuits looked delicious, so we tucked in. Unfortunately, my colleague got his rather large manly forefinger struck in the handle of the cup and while he squirmed, he dropped the biscuit on the carpet leaving a trail of crumbs. I rapidly swept the crumbs under the settee and hissed at him to suck his finger in order to extricate it. There were a few tense moments until he was freed from the cup. It was all I could do to keep a straight face and get out of the house as quickly as possible.

Another challenge when going into people's homes is dealing with the cute or not so cute family pets. I'm allergic to cats and dogs hair, so try to keep my distance, but as you probably know, animals tend to want to investigate strangers in the home. Cats always seemed to walk along the back of the armchair or settee where I was sitting and when ignored would promptly sit down at my shoulder. Within minutes, my eyes would be streaming and I would start sneezing, but would soldier on until I had the required statement and could get back out into the fresh air. I realised that if I wanted to establish rapport with witnesses, then I probably had to appear to like their animals. I don't think antihistamine was widely available then, but I was never prescribed any and just learned to live with my allergies.

Worse still, were the occasions when I would be sitting in someone's home when their dog farted or decided to hump my leg, while everyone in the room kept a straight face and pretended that it wasn't happening. It wasn't easy trying to write a statement with this sort of distraction, but I would finish my work as quickly as possible and try to make a dignified exit. I was sure that other people had enjoyed my discomfort and there would be howls of laughter once I'd gone.

Teamwork was essential, especially when interviewing suspects. The interview rooms were quite Spartan and we didn't have tape recorders, so notes were made contemporaneously. A successful interview usually depended on good investigation, careful planning and good interview technique.

Generally speaking, we worked in pairs and decided which role we would play, with one of us conducting the interview, while the other made the contemporaneous notes. Usually, the male detective would play the part of the hard man by being officious, demanding and piling on the pressure. I would then be left to be more caring and understanding, giving the suspect the chance to unburden themselves. It often worked, but it wasn't always easy pretending to understand the evil ways and vicious acts of some people. Suspects were allowed to ask for a duty solicitor or interpreter, where relevant, and the whole process could take many hours, before deciding to charge or release the prisoner.

Detective officers also regularly carried out prison visits. The purpose was usually to interview a newly convicted prison inmate about similar offences in the area. We used to spend hours trawling through old undetected cases and matching modus operandi (MO) before making a visit.

Bedford prison was right in the town centre, only five minutes' walk from the police station. It had been on this site since 1801 and was quite an imposing building. It has gone down in history for housing some of the most notorious murderers in Britain and for the hanging of James Hanratty on 4 April 1962 for the A6 murder. His was one of the last hangings in Britain, for within three years, capital punishment had been abolished. I don't think one could visit the prison and go behind those massive walls without being aware of a sense of history.

If a detective wanted to visit the prison, we telephoned and made an appointment to see a prisoner. On arrival, we would be checked in and any bags checked. The prisoner would be brought to an interview room and a warder would remain nearby while the interview took place. If the prisoner admitted any additional offences, he would sign a form and the offences would be written off as detected – no proceedings (DNP). The process not only cleared up crimes, but victims found it very reassuring to know that someone had admitted the crime, such as burglary or rape, and was now locked up in prison.

I found prison visits quite intimidating, but often had good results, making it worth the effort. Some of the old lags particularly enjoyed a visit from a female and were only too happy to admit some of their old offences. One prisoner even told me that he would need a week to think about it, so I would have to call again and I obliged. I wasn't a smoker but would buy a packet of cigarettes so that I could offer them to a prisoner during an interview, as I knew that there had to be benefits on both sides.

Sometimes, I was allocated jobs that were rather more bizarre. On one occasion, the Detective Inspector called me into his office as he had a job that required a woman detective. There had been a number of complaints from women about a job that had been advertised in the local newspaper. The advert read 'Young females to train as masseuse for excellent rates of pay'. When applicants telephoned the number, they were offered a job interview at a local hotel. The complainants all stated that they had been compromised and embarrassed during interview. I was to investigate and establish if any offences were committed and take appropriate action.

I telephoned the number given in the advert and arranged to attend the County Hotel for interview. My colleague, DC Keith McCart agreed to come with me and we spoke to the hotel manager. I explained the situation and requested a passkey, which Keith would have to gain access to the room, if he heard me call.

I had been given a room number, so at the appropriate time, knocked on the door. It was opened by a middle-aged man, wearing a dark suit. He greeted me and invited me into the room. He gestured for me to take a seat at one side of a table, while he sat opposite. This was an ordinary hotel bedroom, so there was a double bed at the far side of the room. The interview was conducted in a fairly business-like manner, while the interviewer made notes. Questions were about my previous experience, ability to relate to clients and my expectations from the job. He asked me if I understood what was required from a 'relief massage' and I just nodded my head and smiled. He said that his clients were all professional businessmen, who would be seeking a massage and an hour of pleasurable company. The man then told me that he thought that I would be very suitable for the job, so would like to offer me the post. I thanked him and commented, "The advert said that training would be provided. When will that be?" He replied, "Oh yes, the training. We can do that now". He then stripped off and lay down on the bed saying "Show me what you can do". He was clearly in an aroused state of anticipation. I leant over him and looked him in the eyes, rather than the obvious place. I spoke quietly saying "I can't do this". He said "Why not?" to which I replied, "Because I'm a police officer" and then more loudly "Come in DC McCart". I've never seen a man lose interest so quickly! My colleague came into the room and I then arrested the man for attempting to procure a prostitute under the Sexual Offences Act 1956 and we took him back to the police station.

The interview revealed that the offender was an ordinary businessman. He did not run a masseuse service and did not have any intention of employing young ladies. He had simply devised a cunning plan to regularly rent a hotel room and run mock interviews before inviting girls to provide him with sexual services. They would never hear from him again.

DC McCart and I found the whole incident quite amusing and thought that the offender may well receive a formal caution, but a solicitor was consulted and it was decided that the case should, in the public interest, be taken before a court.

The offender was charged and eventually appeared before the Crown Court, where he was found guilty. He later appealed and the case went before the Court of Appeal, where his conviction was quashed. Apparently, he couldn't be guilty of attempting to procure a common prostitute, because I hadn't ever been a prostitute and was therefore not common! I was quite impressed to have that in writing and felt that at least the man had learned his lesson and would think twice about being a menace to young women. Needless to say, a few of my colleagues asked what my rates were for a massage and were left unsatisfied!

In 1975, there was a report of a missing person, which CID were asked to investigate. It involved a baby of about one year old, who had been taken by its mother, contrary to a court order. She was separated from the father and had been given access to the child, but then ran off with it. There was information that she had gone to London to live in a hippie squat at 1 Cornwall Terrace, a Grade 1 Listed Mansion, overlooking Regent's Park. The neo-classical mansion had been the official residence of the New Zealand High Commissioner from 1955 until the 1970s and had numerous bedrooms, bathrooms, reception rooms and a huge kitchen, but had now been taken over by large numbers of cannabis smoking hippies, who had boarded themselves into the premises and made it a no go area for police and other officials.

As a result it was believed that the missing child could be at risk and a judge had issued a warrant for the child to be located and returned to the father as soon as possible. The Metropolitan Police had been contacted and confirmed details of the hippie squat and said that it would be a major operation to enter the premises on a warrant and they did not have the resources available. Bedfordshire Police also did not have the necessary resources for a raid, so it was suggested that an undercover job would be more successful. My DCI asked me to organise action to recover the child. I was to go to London in a plain car with two male CID colleagues. I dressed as a hippie, wearing old, yellow bell-bottom trousers, a cheesecloth shirt, a well-worn tan coloured suede jacket with shaggy fur edging and platform shoes. My long hair had been left loose, tangled and unwashed for a few days. I probably wasn't scruffy enough, but felt I looked the part. My colleagues were to wait nearby in the car, while I tried to gain access to the house at 1 Cornwall Terrace. I was to try to locate the mother and child, check that the child was in good health and then try to get them to leave the premises. I went up to the front door of the house, which was barricaded with boards and corrugated iron, but saw that there was a gap at the side where two hippies had just left through a window, supposedly to go and get supplies. The window was still insecure so I climbed in and began to wander around the house. The architecture was still impressive, but the condition of the place was almost indescribable. There was no running water, so the palatial bathrooms were filthy and toilets were overflowing. Discarded food containers and wrappings were littered around, as were bottles of alcohol and evidence of drugs, particularly the strong smell of cannabis. There were mattresses, blankets and clothing in most rooms and people lounging around all over the place. Everyone seemed either very laid back or just stoned and I met no resistance. I was nervous, because I was on my own in a very alien environment and hated to think what might have happened to me if they knew that I was a police officer on a mission. I spoke to a young woman who was sober and I said that I had just arrived and was looking for a friend and her baby. She told me where to find them on the first floor, so I followed her directions. The bedroom doors were all open, so it didn't take me long to find the child asleep in a Moses basket and unsupervised. The child fitted the description of the missing baby and the mother was nowhere in sight. My luck was in, so I picked up the baby, which was wrapped in a blanket and calmly walked back through the house and climbed out through the open window. I then ran round the corner to the waiting car and my colleagues and we drove away at speed. I had come prepared to feed and change the baby, so we had no problems on the journey back to Bedfordshire. The child was checked over by a doctor and then handed over to Social Services who took her home to her father.

As for me and my colleagues, we celebrated our success with a few drinks at a local pub. I don't think that we ever heard from the child's hippie mother and to be honest I didn't give her anguish a second thought. It was simply another job well done and within the terms of a legal warrant.

The Metropolitan Police did eventually set up an operation and the squatters were evicted from Cornwall Terrace in the autumn of 1975. The beautiful mansion was subsequently fully restored and sold for millions of pounds.

I eventually made great friends in CID, as I worked long hours, took every job that I could and achieved a high detection rate. I never expected to be treated any differently because I was a woman and if I felt upset or shocked by anything I certainly didn't let anyone know. Occasionally, if a job left me feeling emotional, I shed a few tears privately in the ladies washroom. I didn't ever feel it appropriate to show any weakness in front of my male colleagues, as they all seemed to adopt the stiff upper lip approach. Generally, I was very happy at work and enjoyed the challenges, even when I was dealing with the unusual or felt like a fish out of water.

The theft of vehicles, metals and equipment often required a speedy visit to the local scrap metal dealers, before the goods were crushed and unidentifiable.

One of the experienced detectives took me to a few scrap metal yards, where we spoke to the owners and checked the registers, but after that, I went on my own. I admit to finding these premises quite intimidating and some of the dodgy characters reminded me of the TV programmes 'The Sweeney' and 'Minder' and even 'Steptoe & Son'. Scrap metal dealers were required to keep registers of purchases and record the names and vehicle number of the sellers. There were some honest dealers, but more often, there were cash jobs with no questions asked. This certainly helped to fuel a crime wave that plundered railway cables, copper roofs, sculptures and anything else made of metal, that could fit on the back of a wagon.

During visits, I was definitely out of my comfort zone, but I made sure that I knew the law inside out, which gave me some confidence. At least when I was grinned at and addressed as 'Darling' I could show my warrant card and demand to see records. I knew what I was looking for and would ask relevant questions. Any irregularities would be reported and the dealer could be prosecuted and lose his licence, as well as having suspect items seized.

One of the quirkiest organisations I dealt with, was the Panacea Society of which Bedford is the headquarters. Followers believe that the town will have an important role in the Second Coming of Christ, and is the original location of the Garden of Eden. I'm not so sure about that, but the

Society had some very wealthy, elderly benefactors, around twenty large houses and Victorian villas in Bedford and millions of pounds of assets. Some of the houses in Albany Road, including one known as the Ark were full of priceless artefacts, religious documents and a Pandora style box. Occasionally, there were burglaries and it was quite an experience to attend one of those houses and deal with the crime. Members of the society tended to be genteel, older folk and had to be interviewed in a sensitive way, as they didn't readily talk about the organisation.

Sometimes when artefacts were recovered and officially valued they were found to be worth millions.

I can't say that I alone ever solved any major crimes, but I was part of several murder and rape investigation teams, simply taking statements, carrying out door-to-door enquiries or providing witness support.

The final part of the investigation was the suspect interview, which was usually conducted by senior detectives from HQ. If the case had a successful outcome and prosecution, then there would be quite a celebration up at the police station bar, or at a local pub. On these occasions, I was very much 'one of the boys'.

As a team, we worked hard and played hard, using the typical police black sense of humour to get us through most situations. We also learned to laugh at ourselves and accept a ribbing from our colleagues if we made mistakes. On the other hand, we knew that we would all pull together when the need arose. I remember one such occasion when a colleague had failed to carry out an investigation to the satisfaction of a member of the public. Remedial action was taken, but the man concerned still phoned CID, demanding to see a senior detective in order to make a complaint. The detective who took the call arranged for the complainant to come into the police station at 6.30 pm, when we knew that all the senior officers would be off duty. The CID late team then jumped into action. We each had a part to play in ensuring that the complainant went away satisfied. One of the DCs, who was a tall man with the military bearing of a senior officer, moved into the Detective Chief Inspector's (DCI) office and the rest of us became very deferential. When the complainant arrived, I met him downstairs and brought him up to the DCI's office. I knocked on the door, entered when invited and called my colleague 'Sir'. I introduced the complainant, who was invited to take a comfortable seat. I was asked to bring a tray of tea and then retreated. I heard the raised voice of the complainant and the steady, firm voice of my roleplaying colleague. He then came to the office door and called to another colleague to bring the offending detective to the office. When all the players were in place the 'DCI' could be heard shouting at the detective and telling him that he would 'have his guts for garters' if this ever happened again. He threatened the detective with his job, at which point the complainant said "I really don't think it's necessary to go that far. The officer seems to have learned his lesson!" The detective apologised and then was told to leave, while the 'DCI' and complainant shook hands. As I showed the man back downstairs, he commented that he was very happy with the way that his complaint had been handled and that we were fortunate to have such a fine man in charge. I could not disagree. After all, we had saved the Complaints and Discipline Department a great deal of time and money!

I gained valuable experience and confidence whilst in CID, where I was accepted as one of the team and rather enjoyed having uniformed officers asking me for advice. I began to develop career aspirations, but didn't have a clear plan, as very few posts were open to women.

My book prize from training school, a set of 'Baker & Wilkie Promotion Handbooks' provided me with the motivation to study for the police promotion examination to Sergeant. Men and women took the same exam, which was based on law and procedure in relation to crime, traffic and general police duties.

I think I studied and took the exam simply because I could. I knew that male and female police officers had different career structures and paths to promotion, so I did not expect to be promoted to Sergeant. I never felt satisfied that I knew enough to be good at my job so, although I found it hard to find the time for studying, I found learning immensely satisfying. My character tends to drive me to take on any challenge put in my way. In November 1972, I was delighted when I heard that I had passed the promotion exam to Sergeant, proving that, at least on paper, I was equal.

Chapter 7

Groomed for the Future

It was, apparently, whilst I was in CID, and wearing my favourite white outfit, that PC Mick Groom first really noticed me. He was on patrol in a police car with a male colleague when he saw me walking from the police station to the court building. He told his colleague that I looked gorgeous and had nice legs and wondered who I was. He was duly given my name and informed that I was that same WPC who sometimes worked with the section, but was now with CID.

Soon after that day, I was working in the CID office when I received a call that there had been a rape and the victim was at a phone box near to the scene. I grabbed the only remaining set of keys on the CID keyboard only to find a note saying "Sorry had to dash, car needs refuelling". Somewhat peeved, I rushed to the police station rear yard, jumped into the car and reversed it up to the petrol pump. I put the petrol cap on the roof of the vehicle, while I filled the tank and completed the fuel sheet. I then jumped in the car and drove at speed out of the yard, heading for my assignment. As I turned out of the yard and then took another sharp right hand turn, I noticed in my wing mirror that fuel was spilling from the tank. I realised that in my haste I had not put the fuel cap back on, so I hastily reversed back into the police station yard to look for the cap. Mick Groom strolled over to my vehicle and said, "I thought you would be back for this. I followed you out and picked it up in the road to the left. It was obvious where it would be, the way you swung out to the right at speed." He replaced the petrol cap on my car and said "Now you owe me a favour". I didn't like his manner and I felt like saying "Bloody know all!" but in the circumstances I hadn't got time for banter, so just muttered "Thank you" and quickly drove off. Although the moment's lapse had probably only cost me seconds in time in getting to the job, I was later to find that it would have a major impact on my life.

It was during that summer that to my great delight I was offered tenancy of a council flat in the town centre at Chandos Court, Bedford. I had put my name on the waiting list, but hadn't expected to get allocated a property so soon. I readily accepted and moved into a studio flat on the seventh floor of this fourteen-storey block of flats. My flat consisted of an L-shaped bedroom and lounge, a kitchen and a bathroom. My parents helped me out with a settee, a double bed and a wardrobe. I added a beanbag, a coffee table, a rug and a few posters for the walls. It was all very basic, but I was overjoyed to have my own place, which gave me independence and was so much more convenient than my previous bedsitter accommodation at Park Avenue. There were two lifts in the building and each tenant had a security style intercom connected to the front door, with a telephone connection in the flat. I enjoyed a bachelor girl life style, for the most part enjoying my own company, but occasionally going out on dates, to clubs or inviting friends round for the evening.

I took up the hobby of wine making and regularly had demijohns of various concoctions bubbling away in the airing cupboard. I made some rice and raisin wine, which ended up like Saki and was apparently enjoyed by most of my visitors.

I could not afford to have a telephone installed, so if the police wanted to contact me or call me out for a job, they sent an officer round to my flat. Occasionally, colleagues on patrol would also call around for a cup of coffee and a chat. I was always pleased to see them. I no longer had a landlord to vet my visitors and I was proud to have my own flat, even if it was in a council tower block.

I was at home one evening when the intercom buzzed and I picked up the phone. I heard a voice say, "Hello, it's Mick Groom. Can I come up?" I recognised his voice so I released the door catch and said, "Yes, use the lift to the 7th floor. I will start getting ready". It was my turn on the call-out rota, so I just assumed that Greyfriars needed a female officer.

A few moments later Mick knocked at my door. He was in uniform, so I let him in and invited him to take a seat while I got ready for work. He then said, "It is not a call-out. I just called for coffee. Remember, you owe me a favour from a week ago". I was totally taken aback and thought he had a real cheek. I would only expect colleagues to call if they had a work related purpose, or had been invited as a friend. I knew that my address would be readily available on the call-out rota, but found it hard to believe that he had decided to call on me uninvited. I was rather lost for words and didn't want to be confrontational, so took the easy course of action and made him a coffee. I knew that as he was on duty he couldn't stay long. The conversation was easy going and I found him much more pleasant than I had expected. When he came to leave he said he hoped that he could call again and I was fairly non-committal.

I did not see any more of Mick Groom until about ten days later when I was due to work a late shift with 'C' Section. The section Inspector had asked the Woman Sergeant if a WPC could assist his section with some observations. I was allocated the duty and told to turn up in plain clothes. I subsequently attended the briefing where we were all given our allocated tasks. I was told that I would be on plain-clothes observation with a male constable. We would act as a courting couple and would lay on the riverbank in St. Mary's Gardens, Bedford, adjacent to the river walk and the public toilets. We would be there for several hours, as the observations concerned complaints of gross-indecency in the public toilets.

There was information that male homosexuals regularly used this location to tout for business and this had caused offence to a number of men simply wanting to use the toilets. It was only in 1967 that there had been reforms to the Sexual Offences Act 1967, exempting gay sex from criminal prosecution if sex took place between two consenting males aged twenty one or over in private. A public toilet, however, is not a private place, so when complaints were received, the police had to attempt to crackdown on the unlawful activity by securing evidence of offences.

My job involved going into the ladies' toilet and putting a microphone through a gap in the interior wall into the men's toilets. I was to leave a tape recorder in a ventilator space. I would then return to my position on the river bank, observe and record the description of any men entering the toilets. Other officers would also be keeping observation, using binoculars on the roof of the multi-storey County Hall building, which had a fine view across St. Mary's Gardens. My partner and I would also be required to assist in arrests or securing evidence as necessary and would receive any instructions over police radio. This role seemed fairly normal as women officers were often used in situations such as this where two male officers would look too obvious. The Inspector then read out the name of my partner as PC 142 Groom and I swear that he gave him a knowing smile! Perhaps it was my imagination working and it was just a coincidence that I was to be working with Mick, but I could not help being rather suspicious. After all this was the police service and they regularly played tricks on their colleagues just for fun. I decided to play it cool and just get on with my job, as I would only make a fool of myself if I said anything. It was often quite awkward having to roleplay as a courting couple during observations, especially with someone you didn't fancy, but this was just one of the jobs expected of a policewoman.

After the briefing, I teamed up with Mick, who was also in plain clothes and looked smart in a sports jacket, cord trousers and open necked shirt. We went to St. Mary's Gardens and took up our observation point (OP) near the toilets.

Our colleagues took up their OP on the roof of County Hall and I got the feeling that they would have fun monitoring the behaviour of Mick and me, as well as men visiting the toilets. I went off to put the microphone in the toilets and when I returned Mick had set up the OP with a blanket on the ground!

He also had a flask of coffee and I could not help but feel that at least he was well prepared and we would be comfortable. We settled down on the rug, laying side by side and taking turns to watch the entrance to the toilets. Occasionally it was necessary to snuggle up close, as though we were embracing, to allow one of us to look over the other's shoulder without being too obvious to anyone checking out the area. Apart from that, we were just two colleagues, enjoying a break from normal duties and happily chatting about work and all sorts of topics.

The job went to plan, as we observed various men visiting the public toilets. Some seemed to nip in and out very quickly and raised no suspicions, whereas others entered the toilets separately, at intervals, loitered for twenty minutes and then left looking around rather furtively. They were apprehended and taken to the police station for interview. I retrieved the recording equipment, but am not sure if any prosecutions followed, as I was never called as a witness.

As for me, I had got to know Mick Groom a great deal better and rather unwittingly got more involved with him. When we finished duty that day, he told me that he had enjoyed my company and hoped to see me again soon. I nodded in agreement and he gave me a little kiss on the cheek. I was a bit unsure if this was friendship or being 'chatted up', but I saw no harm in being friendly.

I later found out that Mick was a married man, but he told me that he and his wife were going through a separation. He went to live in the single-men's quarters on the 5th floor of Greyfriars Police Station, so I saw him most days when I was at work and eventually we started a relationship. He was very protective and rather possessive, but at the time I enjoyed his attention. It wasn't long before Mick announced that his divorce had come through and that he was a single man again. I don't remember him ever formally asking me to marry him in a romantic way, but he suggested that as we both had rent allowances that we buy a house together. We had to formally ask permission to do so and this was granted. We bought our first home, an end terraced modern house down by the river in Queens Park, Bedford.

We enjoyed being a couple and treated ourselves to a number of cheap long-weekend holidays in Spain and Majorca. Foreign travel was still a novelty for most working class people and our bargain weekend breaks with Clarkson's were only about £30 each, including airfare and half board! Mick started to organise group holidays to Spain for his entire section during long weekends off duty. We had four such trips until the Superintendent heard about them and insisted that it stop. Apparently, this was for operational reasons, because if the plane crashed, it would be difficult for the police service to manage without a whole section of officers. Mick and I had to obey orders, but occasionally still managed to travel as a couple on cheap trips abroad mainly to Spain or Greece.

After applying to the Chief Constable for permission, Mick and I were married at Bedford Register Office on 23rd February 1973. It was a very low-key affair attended by my parents and a few friends, followed by a party at our house. As Mick was a divorcee and we had limited finances, I didn't wear white and just bought a turquoise and white suit and a big hat, from budget retailers C&A. I was happy to get married and become Mrs Groom.

Although Mick and I had both received rent allowances while we were just living together, as soon as we married, this was reduced to half each. Our combined wages still meant that we could afford to pay a small mortgage, but there wasn't much left for luxuries and we certainly couldn't afford to have children at that time. That wasn't a problem as I was content to carry on enjoying my career and at least I had a husband who understood the rigours of shift work and long hours.

Chapter 8

Stripes & Equality

Although I had been delighted when I passed the police promotion exam to Sergeant, I didn't really expect promotion, as opportunities for women were very limited. Equal opportunities had not yet arrived within general policing, so regardless of being treated as an equal in CID, promotion would mean returning to the policewomen's department. Promotion boards didn't exist at that time, so I decided to put the idea of promotion to the back of my mind and carry on enjoying work as a detective.

Then, in January 1973, much to my surprise, I was promoted to Sergeant. The news came just as I was boarding a coach in front of the police station to travel to Spain for a long weekend with Mick, and a group of police colleagues. The coach was kept waiting while I was called back into the police station to see the Chief Superintendent. I thought I had done something wrong, so was delighted when, on entering his office, the Chief Superintendent called me 'Sergeant' and told me to go and celebrate with my friends. I certainly fulfilled that order to the full!

Following my promotion and my marriage, I collected my new warrant card and became Woman Sergeant 1311

Groom. My first Sergeant's role was back in the Policewomen's Department, as there were no other Sergeants' posts open to women. As a Woman Sergeant I was again specialising in tracing missing persons and offences involving women and children. It was a new challenge being a supervisor, but I missed my male colleagues and the wider challenge of work in CID. Nonetheless, I realised that I was very fortunate to have achieved the rank of Sergeant with only three years of police experience, so decided to make the most of the opportunity.

I continued to study and in January 1974 I passed the Promotion exam to Inspector, but knew that the chances of being promoted further were very slim. The highest rank achieved by a woman in Bedfordshire Police was Inspector, but that was within the Policewomen's Department and there were no vacancies. Besides which, I was married to a PC, who supported me in my studies, but had no desire at that time to further his own career. I was already one rank above him and I wasn't sure how it would affect our relationship if I sought further promotion. At least while I was working in the Policewomen's Department, there was no professional conflict when we were at work.

It was however, a time of major change in the police service and I would find it difficult to ignore a challenge. The Equal Pay Act 1970 had not had an impact on policewomen's salaries, as it was considered that policewomen's specialist work was different from patrol duties performed by our male colleagues. As a result, in 1974, women were still receiving only seven-eighths of the men's salary, even though male officers in office jobs or specialist departments were not similarly affected.

In 1975, however, a European Union Directive and the Sex Discrimination Act would have an impact on equal opportunities in the work place, ensuring that all officers of the same rank would receive the same basic salary.

I pre-empted the legal requirements concerning the deployment of officers, as in July 1974, I became aware that Bedfordshire Police was suffering from manpower shortages. There were budget restrictions, a freeze on recruiting and restrictions on overtime, so the operational sections were stretched to the limit. I realised that this could be an opportunity for greater integration of policewomen, so I submitted a report to Chief Constable, suggesting that women officers be utilised to meet the shortfall on the men's sections.

Needless to say, he agreed and throughout the county, many of the WPCs began to work on the patrol sections. I was delighted to be working as a Sergeant on general police duties, but I did realise that not all the women officers were happy with the changes, especially as they now had to work shifts. The Force didn't have any married women officers with children, so I couldn't foresee any real problems and knew that, with forthcoming equal pay, women would be required to work the same hours as the men.

On the first day of going out on general patrol in a panda car, the press arrived at the station to conduct an interview with me and my colleague Joan Wright. The press headline later read 'Women's Lib on the Force.' I certainly didn't see this as 'Women's Lib', but it was a big step forward in achieving equal opportunities.

At about the same time, women officers were issued with smart new uniforms, which had been designed by Norman Hartnell, who also designed a similar style for air hostesses. Initially, we still had to wear skirts, but with a double-breasted box jacket and a pork pie shaped hat with polished peak. We now had shirts with collars attached and a bow tie on an elastic neckband. These were later replaced with a clip-on style for safety reasons. The uniform was smart, feminine and comfortable, but still impractical for active police duties, such as climbing over walls or wrestling with a prisoner. A handbag was still issued to every woman officer.

When we started to work night shifts, it was eventually agreed that trousers could be worn on night duty or in very cold weather. If attending court or on normal day shifts, skirts would still be worn. The initial batch of uniform issue trousers, were not designed for women's figures. They were ill-fitting and rejected by many women, who then bought their own.

As anticipated, by 1975, women police were fully integrated into police duties, with the majority working on the twenty-four-hour shift pattern. We also received equal pay with our male colleagues. It was decided that we would no longer be referred to as WPCs and would be PC or Sergeant, in the same way as our male colleagues. In order to be able to differentiate for operational reasons, all female constables were given numbers within the nine hundreds, for example: number 6 became 906.

Some women were retained in specialist departments, now called Juvenile Liaison and Social Enquiry Departments. They continued using their expertise, dealing with specialist work involving women and children, but they now had some male colleagues in the department. This seemed eminently sensible as some male officers were husbands and fathers and brought a great deal of experience to the role.

A small number of women officers were not at all happy with the changes and left the police service. Others were initially apprehensive about the changes, but soon adapted to their new role.

Some male officers, who had previously been quite protective of WPCs, now were less chivalrous at fights or when a job required physical strength and made comments such as "You asked for equal opportunities and equal pay and now you've got it!" Generally speaking though, most of us acknowledged that there were 'horses for courses'. We all had different strengths and abilities, which worked well as part of a team and some of my female colleagues, were stronger and fitter than their male counterparts.

Following integration, I had various Sergeants roles, such as Patrol Sergeant, Station Sergeant, Rural Area Sergeant, Custody Officer and Court Prosecutor. The variety of work was endless, one day enjoying talking to parishioners in a local village and another day dealing with a pub fight, or receiving prisoners at the custody suite.

In Bedford urban area, we worked shifts of 6am – 2pm (early turn), 2pm – 10pm (late turn) and 10pm – 6am (nights). On each shift there was usually a duty Inspector, a Station Sergeant, two Patrol Sergeants and about ten officers to cover the North Bedfordshire area either on mobile patrol, town centre foot beats or station duties.

Officers usually patrolled alone, but had personal radios to contact local control at the police station. In some areas the signal broke up, so we had to be independent and resourceful. Cars were also fitted with more reliable Very High Frequency (VHF) radios, which were on a county-wide frequency and controlled from police HQ.

General police duties included attending crimes such as thefts, burglaries and assaults, road traffic accidents, fights, public disorder and domestics. We also dealt with missing persons, sudden deaths, drugs and driving offences.

The Road Safety Act of 1967 had introduced new drink driving offences and a blood/alcohol limit, so all cars carried a breathalyser kit and these were well used.

The Patrol Sergeant's job was very hands on, attending incidents, prioritising jobs and providing back-up, as necessary. We then supervised the interview of prisoners, collection of evidence and the submission of reports.

During the day, there were always a number of senior officers on duty at the police station, some of whom were strict disciplinarians. They had all started as constables and worked their way through the ranks so, although we didn't realise it at the time, they tended to know every trick in the book and certainly didn't miss much. It was not unusual to hear a PC being shouted at for some minor infringement of police regulations, such as loitering around the police station or having been seen out on patrol when not wearing his helmet or cap. There was also an occasion when one of our section officers received a dressing down from the Chief Inspector for wearing his helmet in an unusual manner. He had been spotted with his helmet balanced rather precariously on his head, while he wandered around on foot patrol with a glazed expression on his face. The Chief Inspector had noticed the PC suddenly get excited and give a celebratory punch in the air. Upon investigation, he had discovered that the officer had a transistor radio under his helmet and was listening to the cricket scores. The Chief Inspector had confiscated the radio and said "I'll see you in my office!" Those of us who were working at the police station were much amused when we heard the Chief Inspector bellowing threats at the unfortunate PC. We knew that we would be laughing together in the bar that evening. According to stories that I heard, police helmets were very popular items of uniform with the beat Bobby, as their shape could accommodate a pork pie or pack of sandwiches!

One of our PCs seemed to be prone to having minor accidents in his police patrol car and the Superintendent was adamant that he would discipline the officer and suspend him from driving if he damaged another police vehicle. There was an instruction to the PC that if, for any reason, he had so much as a scratch on the car, he was to call for a Sergeant to attend the incident and submit a full report with supporting evidence. One evening, I subsequently got the call to attend a road traffic incident involving this PC. He was on the rural outskirts of the town and said that a small Muntjac Deer had run in front of the car and struck the bonnet, before running into the undergrowth. There was a dent in the bonnet of the car, so I completed an accident form and we then searched the undergrowth and found the deceased deer. I knew that the Superintendent would not believe the explanation, so we used one of the accident signs from the car as a sling and lifted the deer into the boot of the car. We returned to the rear yard of the police station and took the deer into the police garage where the Superintendent had his own allocated parking bay. The dead animal was arranged in a seated position in the bay with a label around its neck saying 'Evidence of road traffic accident involving police car'. We knew that the Superintendent would be furious when he arrived the next morning and couldn't park his car in the bay, but it seemed worth the risk and we both went home with grins on our faces. I was then off duty for two days which gave the Chief Inspector time to calm down. When he next saw me he just said, "You're pushing your luck Sergeant!" and with a big smile I replied, "Sorry Sir". I think it's true to say that, as a female, I did get away with rather more than my male colleagues. Although women were regarded as the weaker sex, I soon learned that the male ego can be rather a fragile thing and was usually not averse to a bit of flattery.

There was always a great team spirit on the section, rather like a big family, and we all looked after each other, especially when there was a fight or car chase. We all enjoyed the excitement and adrenalin flow and even when sufficient resources had been allocated, it was always a challenge for supervisors to hold the others back. We generally lived by the premise that out on the streets, we didn't let the villain get away with crime and if they attacked us, we gave as good as we got! Once a prisoner was in custody and brought into the police station however, custody rules applied. If the prisoner was still in fighting mood or generally non-compliant, he would be placed in a cell until he calmed down. A prisoner could call for a solicitor, a doctor, an interpreter, or phone a friend before we started interviewing, so it could be a long drawn-out process, which committed police resources.

Drunken revellers were a cause of annoyance and a waste of police resources, especially at weekends in the area of Bedford High Street, so we maintained foot patrols and a van in the area, particularly between 10pm – 2am. We dispersed the noisy revellers and drunks coming out of the pubs and clubs, and dealt with any fights, and then the streets returned to normal.

One pet hate I have, is men who come out of the pub having had a 'skin full' of beer and then pee in shop doorways. When I was on foot patrol in the town centre I used to wait quietly in the shadows until a man was in full flow and then tap him on the shoulder. It is amazing how the sight of a police officer and stern words of advice can redirect the flow straight down the offender's trouser leg!

Sometimes offences were more bizarre and rather more serious. One evening, we noticed a crowd gathering outside Debenhams display window. A drunken male had taken a fancy to one of the female mannequins and had broken in through the loading bay. He was in the window display, trying to have sex with the mannequin, much to the amusement of passers-by.

Section officers came into the canteen on the 4th floor for either early or late refreshments, about half way through the shift. From that vantage point, we had a good view of the bus station and multi-storey car park opposite. We sometimes spotted attempted suicides at the multi-storey car park, road traffic accidents, drunken brawls or crimes and would immediately dispatch officers to deal with the incident. The rest of us would monitor the situation on our radios, while finishing off our food or game of cards, but would be prepared to rush off at a moment's notice.

This car park was also the scene of what was known as the 'police cycle proficiency test'. If it was quiet during the early hours of the morning, new recruits who wanted to ride a police cycle instead of walking, were taken over to the multi-storey for a 'cycle proficiency test'.

This involved riding down the circular ramps of the multi-storey car-park. The young officer would be told that it was a time trial, so usually risked life and limb to get to the bottom quickly. On arrival at ground level, he would be greeted by colleagues, howling with laughter.

By about 3am, if it was quiet, foot beat officers, mainly Probationer Constables, would be out checking property around the town. Occasionally, there were problems with security or an alarm going off, and we would call out a key holder, but often it remained eerily quiet. This was another opportunity to test out the mettle of young officers.

Above the town, there was a network of roof top walks and fire escapes, often with metal bars between two premises. Sometimes, one of the old stagers would position himself above an alleyway with a shop dummy on a rope. The unsuspecting rookie would get a call to check out a suspected burglary at specific premises. Even with a torch, it can seem rather spooky in some of the alleyways and, as the young officer approached, the shop dummy would suddenly drop down on a rope or fall out of a doorway. Even the bravest soul might let out a wail or scream before hearing the laughter from colleagues

These initiation tests seemed like huge fun at the time and by using local UHF radio control we could ensure that HQ remained oblivious. Although we were professionals doing a serious and sometimes difficult job, we all learned to laugh at ourselves and as a result of a shared joke, the section bonded as a team. These initiations wouldn't be allowed to happen today and as a result, it's probably a safer, more sterile environment, but a lot less fun!

My role as a Patrol Sergeant in Bedford included encouraging initiative in the new probationer constables. One of my team had been passing a run-down house on his beat when he noticed that the windows were all steamed up. Although the curtains were drawn, he noted that there were lights on inside, so he peered in a back window and saw lots of plants growing inside. After enquiries and consultation with the drug squad, it was believed that cannabis was being grown using hydroponics. Instead of growing plants in soil, hydroponics utilizes solutions or a medium filled with minerals and then adds warmth and light to nourish plants.

We took out a warrant and raided the premises and found every room in the house being used for growing cannabis. The officer's early initiative led to a good drugs haul and a successful court case and we were all delighted for him. A success for one officer was viewed as a success for the team and called for a celebration at the bar.

Bedford urban area was and still is an ethnically and linguistically diverse town with many different nationalities: Italians, Poles, a large Asian population and black community, mainly from the Caribbean. Generally speaking, everyone lived in relative harmony, although there were occasionally cross cultural challenges. I enjoyed working in this environment and tried very hard to understand the various cultures and religions.

In the 1970s, a few houses in the Queens Park area of Bedford served as temples and mosques. Forty years later, there are four mosques and the largest Sikh temple in the United Kingdom outside London.

As a Sergeant, I would make regular liaison visits, often with the local beat Bobby or a Probationer Constable and it was essential to know the customs and taboos.

Wherever possible, I would try to respect the beliefs and values of others, but I did sometimes feel at a disadvantage, being a Woman Sergeant, as this did not sit easily with some cultural norms. On the other hand, I had a job to do, especially if we were investigating a crime or a missing person, so I just had to brazen it out and make it quite clear that I had authority to take action if necessary.

The 1970s and 1980s were the heyday of Rastafarian Reggae singer Bob Marley. Bedford was home to a number of Rastafarians, who had their own culture and style of dress, including hair in dreadlocks. Rastafarians were generally peaceful, but tended to be anti-authority. This sometimes led to confrontation, especially concerning smoking and dealing in Marijuana.

As a new section Patrol Sergeant on a predominately male section, I knew that some of the men were waiting for me to prove myself and an unexpected opportunity arose. I was on patrol, driving the police van with young PC as passenger, when we stopped some Rastafarians, who we suspected of being involved in minor crime. I parked the van while the PC got out, intending to talk to the group. As soon as he approached, three of the men ran away, but one of them kicked the PC between the legs and he fell to the ground in agony. The offender was about to run, but I arrested him for assaulting a police officer and took hold of his arm. He struggled so violently that the sleeve tore from his woollen jacket. He was six feet tall and strong and I feared that I would lose him, as I couldn't get him into a restraining hold. He tried to kick me, so I grabbed a handful of his dreadlocks to keep his head down. As we struggled the dreadlocks came away in my hand. He was still trying to kick me, so I reached down and grabbed hold of the most delicate part of his anatomy and squeezed tight. He stood on his toes, remained very still and had a pained, startled look on his face. I then managed to push the button on my radio and request assistance. A police van arrived within minutes and as they opened the back doors of the van two of my PCs said, "Do you want any help Serge?" In reply I just kept my hold on the prisoner and threw him in. We returned to Greyfriars police station, where he was charged and later convicted at court for several offences, but there was also another outcome for me. In those days we used to parade our section on duty and check uniform and equipment were in order. The following afternoon, as I went along the line, instead of standing to attention, all my male officers had their hands protecting their private parts and big grins on their faces. Word had clearly got around that I was prepared to play dirty if necessary and from that day on, I never had any problems with discipline!

There's always lots of variety in police work. One evening, there was a radio call asking for an officer to attend a threatened suicide, where a woman was believed to be drowning herself in a bath. All my officers were committed, so I took the call and attended the scene at a Victorian house in Ashburton Road. The lady had apparently locked the front door and gone up to the third floor of the house and locked herself in the bathroom. I knocked on the front door, but there was no reply, so after checking the back door and ground floor windows, I tried to shoulder open the front door, but it was heavy oak and wouldn't budge. It always looks a lot easier on films!

The third floor bathroom window was of a sash type and partially open. An onlooker said that there was an extended ladder at the house next door where renovations were taking place. Time was of an essence, so I agreed with his suggestion and two men brought the ladder round. There were volunteers to hold the ladder, but not to climb up. Everyone seemed to have confidence in me, so I duly started to climb up. I don't particularly like heights and the ladder seemed to be swaying as I got higher, but I was more concerned about the fact that I was wearing a skirt and tights and onlookers were probably getting an eyeful. Eventually, I got level with the window, which was partially open at the bottom, but was stuck in that position. I could just see a woman in bath with her head under the water and the tap running, flooding the floor. I decided to squeeze through the gap under the window. I hitched my skirt up and got my leg and shoulder through, but then got stuck. To my embarrassment the gusset of my tights was caught up on the window catch. There was no choice but to tear myself free by throwing myself through the window. The bottom literally fell out of my world as I skidded across the wet floor. I pulled the woman from the bath, but could not resuscitate her. While I waited for the doctor and the Coroners Officer I removed my tattered tights and tried to recover my dignity. Not all our jobs had successful outcomes, but we could but try our best.

Each officer was trusted to use their discretion in how they tackled a job and whether or not they did so alone or waited for back-up. Health and safety was not uppermost in our minds and all officers occasionally put themselves at risk to get the job done, be it dealing with a violent prisoner, entering a dangerous situation or trying to save someone else's life. Most of us suffered a few cuts and bruises at various times in our careers, but serious injuries fortunately were rare and in the culture of the day it was not the done thing to make a fuss. If an officer put out a radio call to say that they needed assistance, then every available resource would attend. It was the Sergeant's job to take control and reallocate resources as necessary.

On one occasion, all my officers were committed on jobs and there was a radio call requesting an officer to attend a house in Bedford, where an escaped mental patient had gone to visit his sister, but now wanted to hand himself in to the police. I took the job and attended the address where the man was reported to be. I knocked on the front door and waited patiently, not expecting any trouble, but the door was flung open and a man came at me with a carving knife. He was six foot tall, heavy built and looked absolutely wild with staring eyes. I managed to back away and realised that there was no way that I could overpower this man or have time to make a radio call. My heart was racing and I was frightened, but somehow managed to sound calm as I tried to convince him that he wouldn't want to harm a woman and then talked him round to throwing down the knife. I was relieved when he threw it down at my feet, but I hastily picked it up in case he changed his mind. I was then able to call for assistance on the radio and escort the man back to the mental hospital, where he was officially detained under a Mental Health Order. I was initially rather shaken by the incident, as the violence had been unanticipated, but I was lucky not to be hurt and soon found myself laughing about the incident with colleagues.

At the end of our tour of duty, all officers, other than those dealing with incidents, reported to the parade room. There would be a quick debrief by the Inspector or Sergeant, before going off duty. As the next section arrived to parade on duty, there was a handover of car keys and essential information, but there was also a healthy, good-natured rivalry between the sections.

At the end of 1977, there was a nine-week national strike by the Firemen's Union. The government called upon armed forces to provide cover, using the old Green Goddess fire engines. Local police worked in liaison, providing a pilot car to direct them with speed and safety to the scene of any fire. In Bedford, the Green Goddesses were stationed at the Territorial Army (TA) Centre in Ashburton Road.

At Christmas, as duty Sergeant on the late shift, I was asked to call at the TA Centre and see the Army Commanding Officer. He told me that he had a problem in that our local Charles Wells Brewery had been very generous and donated barrels of beer for the lads, but they simply couldn't drink it all. He asked if we could take a few barrels off their hands, so I obliged!

I arranged for our van with its driver, a discreet old stager, to attend, and barrels of mild and bitter were duly installed in the back of the van with a box of pint glasses. We then made our way around foot patrols, wishing them a Merry Christmas. I acted in a formal manner as I checked and signed each officer's pocket book and then my driver invited the officer round the back of the van for a drop of festive cheer. Between visits, we received a call for the van to attend a fight in the High Street and we speedily made our way there with blue lights flashing. We sorted out a minor skirmish, being careful not to make any arrests and then returned to our more festive role. The next officer to have a drink had quite a frothy head on his beer!

I had a great section of dedicated men and women, who worked very hard, but as a section we also made the most of our social life and were like one big family.

I enjoyed life as a section Sergeant in the urban area, but in the police service most officers get moved around every few years and I was moved to duties on a rural area. I soon found out that there were benefits, because I realised that, as a rural Sergeant with a team of neighbourhood officers and rural patrol cars, I had chance to really get to know members of the community. I attended Parish Council meetings, helped to plan action to deal with local problems and really felt that our team could make a difference. I also gave talks to local groups such as the Scouts, Women's Institute, Parent Teacher Organisations and the Rotary.

Rural life also had its more unusual challenges. At training school we had learned about Epizootic Lymphangitis, Foot and Mouth & other diseases of animals, which I never thought I would refer to again. In

1972 however, as a Rural Sergeant for North Bedfordshire, I automatically became the Diseases of Animals Inspector and when there was an outbreak of Swine Vesicular Disease, I had to learn very quickly about isolation and movement of animals' restrictions. It must have been obvious to the farmers that I was an ignorant 'townie' but they humoured me and gave me a modicum of respect as I tried to do my job.

Late one evening I was on patrol in the rural area of Ravensden, North Bedfordshire, when I saw a number of lights flashing in a nearby field. I called the radio controller to check if there were other resources in the area, but there was a negative response, so I advised the controller that I would investigate on foot and report back in fifteen minutes. I parked the police car behind some trees and followed a track towards the lights. I came across a Land Rover, made a note of the registration number and informed the radio controller. Then, nervously clutching a heavy metal torch, I walked further along the path and came up behind a group of four men. Two of them were carrying shotguns and I thought they all might be gypsies caught in the act of poaching. I turned on the powerful beam of my torch and shouted "Police. You are surrounded. Stay where you are!" They stood still and turned to shine their lights on me and I spoke to the oldest one of the four, asking him if they had permission to be on the land and licenses for the shotguns. To my surprise he answered in a Bedfordshire accent, but very politely, telling me that he was the farmer and landowner and that his documents were all at home. As none of the four men had any identification on them, I told them to get in the vehicle and drive to the farm house, while I followed in my car. They obliged and I breathed a sigh of relief, as I knew that I could have ended up in trouble if these men had been villains. On the other hand, it would have seemed cowardly to drive past and not investigate. On arrival at the farmhouse, the men all went inside and the farmer called to his wife to put the kettle on. She came into the kitchen in her dressing gown and on seeing me, said "Maurice, you silly sod, what have you been up to now?" He explained that he had decided to go 'lamping' with a few friends (startling rabbits with bright lights and then shooting them) and then I had turned up. He laughed about me saying that they were surrounded and said "You've certainly got plenty of nerve girl!" I think that was a compliment, although I realised that my actions must have seemed rather bizarre. After checking his documents and advising radio control that all was in order, I then relaxed for a while with the farmer and his wife and was even given a tour of the farmhouse and its very fine wine cellar and game store. It turned out that the farmer was one of the biggest landowners in North Bedfordshire and he was impressed to think that the local police would check out poachers on his land. I was invited to call for coffee whenever I was passing and eventually my husband and I became good friends with the farmer and his family.

Rural life also had some tasty advantages. If our officers attended an accident involving a deer, the clean-up process required the removal of the carcase. Luckily, a member of our section was an ex-butcher, so the meat was delivered to his garage and in due course he would arrive at the station with a bounty of venison steaks. 'Waste not, want not!'

Bedfordshire is a market gardening area, so when there was a seasonal glut of fruit and vegetables, it wasn't unusual for the local Bobby or area car to be given a share of the bounty. It was against the rules but seemed just part of rural life. The trouble was that on a busy day you sometimes ended up riding around with the forbidden fruit in the boot of the car and Brussels sprouts and strawberries really stink on a hot day!

On the subject of 'forbidden freebies' there was one incident that came to the attention of the local press and became known as the Quality Street Gang.

Traffic officers attended a motorway incident where a lorry had turned over and spilled its load. They were greeted with a road strewn with Quality Street. The tins were damaged or dented and after consulting his firm, the driver said that the whole load was to be written off. He asked if the police officers would like some. Word went out and very soon police cars appeared and tidied up the scene. Being generous sorts, they then shared them with all their colleagues, even taking some round to officers who were on leave. We missed out on our section but were quite relieved when a member of the public reported seeing officers putting the sweets in a car. It is against the Discipline Code to receive reward or remuneration, so an enquiry was instigated. The company did not want to pursue the matter and the enquiry established that there were too many officers involved to discipline them all. There were a number of warnings and the matter was laid to rest but never forgotten.

For two years, I performed the role of Station Sergeant, which included the role of Custody Officer. Male prisoners were often surprised to see a young female Sergeant in charge, but it usually had a calming effect. I think that maybe an assertive female simply reminded them of the wife or mother waiting to nag them at home!

The worst part of the Custody Sergeant's job was starting the early shift at 5.45 am. Before accepting responsibility, we would check the prisoners in the cells and this needed a strong constitution. Both the men's and the women's cells were not a pretty sight and the smell was appalling!

I enjoyed the challenging and demanding role of Custody Sergeant and appreciated how important it was to get the station procedures right if we were going to gain a conviction at court. It was my decision as to whether to release, charge a prisoner, or to grant bail, pending ongoing enquiries. I saw the full spectrum of human life in this job, from decent people who had made a big mistake and got involved in criminal behaviour, to career criminals who had no respect for anyone and no remorse for the crimes they had committed. Suspects of all ages and persuasions came through the custody process, including thieves, murderers, rapists and child molesters. Regardless of my own personal feelings, the job demanded that they were afforded their rights and treated as innocent until found guilty before a court.

Usually, when a man was arrested for a violent rape, I had already seen the distressed victim at the police station, so it was hard to stay impartial, especially if the man was arrogant, foul mouthed or violent. As part of the investigation, I usually arranged for a police doctor to examine the suspect and take any necessary samples, which included pubic hair. If the doctor asked me if the sample should be cut with scissors or plucked, I always got some small satisfaction by answering 'plucked!'

On one occasion, I was Custody Sergeant, when a group of travellers were brought into the police station after being arrested for theft and assault on the arresting officers. The group included three men and two women who had been living on an unofficial travellers' site at Cutthroat Lane, off Clapham Road, Bedford. The site was notorious for crime and a team of officers had gone there to recover stolen property and make the arrests. Having found the evidence, the officers arrested the three male suspects, but were then set upon by the women, who were quite vicious. They had no choice but to also arrest the two women, but then three children came out of one of the caravans and started throwing bricks at the officers and police vans, causing quite a lot of damage. The children were simply following the parents' example, but were uncontrollable and could not be left alone on the site, so were also bundled into the van and brought to the police station as a place of safety. They were aged about five, seven and nine and looked like dirty little street urchins. They looked like they needed a good wash and their clothes were dirty and had holes in them.

When they arrived at the police station, the children were more subdued. I contacted Social Services to advise them of the situation, but there was no temporary place available for the children, so it was agreed that they would have to remain at the police station until their parents were interviewed and a decision made about charges, custody or release. This procedure would take hours and I certainly didn't want the added burden of caring for three unruly children in a busy custody area. The children were taken to a juvenile detention room and a policewoman posted at the door, which was left partly open. I spoke to their mother and explained the situation and allowed her to visit the children to reassure them, before she returned to a cell.

The children became very quiet, huddled together under a blanket and looked so vulnerable that my heart went out to them. I then surprised officers on my section by showing my maternal instincts instead of my usual business-like approach. I sent an officer to the supermarket to buy children's bubble bath, crayons and colouring books. Meanwhile I telephoned the Salvation Army to ask if they had suitable clothes and shoes for the children and they came up trumps with a good selection.

I then filled one of the baths in the cellblock with warm water and bubble bath and took the children to the bathroom for a wash. I don't think they had ever seen a big bath, but it wasn't long before their childish curiosity took over and they were stripped off, enjoying a bath. It was delightful to hear them laughing as they played in the bubbles and had their hair washed. After getting dried they were offered a choice of new clothes and it was like watching excited children on Christmas morning. They returned to the detention room looking like totally different children, but I probably looked more dishevelled than usual. We ordered them food from the police canteen and they tucked in with gusto. I then put on a very stern act as I gave them the colouring books and crayons and told them what would happen if they dared to write on the walls! My colleagues and I were then able to get on with our work while the children settled down to a colouring session.

One of my PCs said, "I don't know why you bother Sergeant. They were throwing bricks at us. They're travellers' kids and will soon revert to type". Perhaps, all my section thought I'd gone soft, but to me these were just children and I didn't think it did any harm to let them see that police officers could be kind and decent. When they eventually left the police station with their mother, they were clutching their colouring books and one of them smiled and politely said "Good bye, Miss"

At 2am one morning, I was having my refreshments in the 4th floor canteen. On looking out the window I saw a light flashing at the bus station photo booth, so I dispatched two officers to go and check it out. Ten minutes later the officers called on the radio to say they were bringing in a prisoner. I went to the custody suite to await their arrival. The officer said that on approaching the kiosk he had observed the light flashing. The curtain was drawn and on the revolving seat, he saw a man's feet with trousers and pants round his ankles. He appeared to be taking naked photos of himself. The officers pulled back the curtain and helped the man from his perch. He was arrested for indecency offences in a public place but denied any offence. The officers then waited for three minutes until the evidential photos arrived. These were now produced and handed to me. After carefully studying the photos and looking the prisoner up and down, I then commented that the evidence was unacceptable as the item was very underdeveloped. The hapless offender looked embarrassed and then we all burst out laughing. At that time of the morning, he had not offended any member of the public, so was given an informal warning and sent on his way with his photographs as a keepsake!

As Station Sergeant I was in charge of the found property store. Sometimes in the early hours of morning, I kept myself awake by checking the property against the register. Occasionally, this also provided entertainment. Skateboards were fairly new on the scene and I'd never tried one. When one was handed in as found property and I was taking it down to the basement store, I decided to have a go on it. We had a rifle range in the basement so there was a long smooth concrete floor, which seemed like the perfect surface. I thought I was just getting the hang of skateboarding, when the door opened and two of the station staff peeped round. They were just in time to see me take a tumble. There was no sympathy, just laughter, as I ended up on my backside. They apparently knew that I wouldn't be able to resist trying it.

I was however much better at roller-skating, so when an old adjustable pair was handed in we decided to have a station challenge. Greyfriars Police Station had a corridor the full length of the ground floor with the Enquiry Office at one end and the men's toilets at the other. The competition was staged between 2 am and 5 am. We each put £1 in the hat and the winner would take all. When my turn came, I powered down the corridor, reached the end and touched the toilet door, which crashed open to reveal a man at the urinal. Hooting with laughter, I turned round and headed back up the corridor. Unknown to me, an irate member of the public came into the Enquiry Office demanding to speak to the officer in charge. The enquiry officer said "Certainly Sir, I'll ask her to get her skates on!" and within seconds I arrived. I may have looked a bit hot and bothered, but simply took the skates off and said "How can I help you Sir". That took the wind right out of his sails. I sorted out his problem and he left looking bemused!

One of my less enjoyable county roles was when I was in charge of a sector at Luton Football Ground, Kenilworth Road. I've never been a football fan and hated all the traffic disruption and public disorder that so often occurred. I was much happier on duties outside the ground, while the match was in progress. With my unit, I patrolled the area and waited for the fans to emerge after the match. The tactic was to keep opposing fans apart, to limit the opportunity for fighting. I would receive a radio message when the match ended and the gates were about to open. Then, the away fans emerged in a sudden rush. We would form a cordon around away supporters and escort them straight down to the railway station where special trains were laid on. British Transport Police would then take over. Other away supporters were escorted straight to their coaches parked outside the grounds. Generally speaking, the tactics worked and we kept the fans apart. Sometimes tempers frayed and the away fans wanted to stay and fight. I remember one occasion when they refused to get on the coaches and started pulling the coping bricks off the garden walls to use as missiles. As soon as the bricks started flying, we called in the police dogs and they soon got things organised. You've never seen people get on coaches so fast, as the police dogs snapped at their backsides. I think at least eighty people got on a sixty-seat coach!

As I reached my thirties, I was still enjoying all the variety, challenges and fun of life in the police service. My appraisal reports said that I was a good Sergeant, demonstrating practical ability and leadership qualities. I had certainly grown in confidence and now felt very comfortable in my supervisory role, so I was now ready for a new challenge.

Special Constable Hertfordshire, 1966

The Pines Bedford Police HQ, 1969
(By kind permission of Bedfordshire Police)

Chief Constable Henry Pratt, 1969
(By kind permission of Bedfordshire Police)

Police Training Centre at Ryton on Dunsmore, 1969

Ryton Initial Training, 1969

Passing out parade Ryton on Dunsmore, July 1969

*Greyfriars Police Station, Bedford
(By kind permission of Bedfordshire Police)*

My favourite foot beat – Bedford Embankment

Continuation Course – Bruche Regional Training Centre,
October 1970

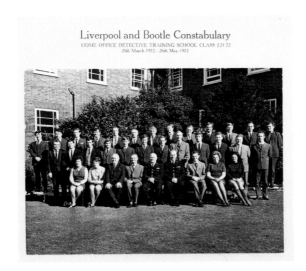

CID Course at Liverpool, March 1972

Promoted to Woman Sergeant, January 1973

Unit Beat Policing and Mini Panda Cars
(By kind permission of Bedfordshire Police)

Carole & Joan – 1st General Patrol, 1974
(By kind permission of Bedford Times & Citizen)

Police cell corridor

Police cell. Custody Sergeant Duty

Prosecutor Duties at Bedford Court

Rural Sergeant
(By kind permission of Bedfordshire Police)

Daughter Michelle born May, 1981

129

Schools Liaison

Unofficial training session with Bedfordshire Police Search & Recovery Team

Diving with Bedfordshire Police Search & recovery Team

Groom family, 1984

Police Instructors Course Harrogate, 1984

Police Long Service & Good Conduct Medal Ceremony
(Photo by kind permission of Bedfordshire police)

Training Dept at HQ
(By kind permission of Bedfordshire police)

Bedfordshire Police HQ
(By kind permission of Bedfordshire Police)

Race Relations Training at Police Staff College at Bramshill

Biggleswade Police Station
(By kind permission of Bedfordshire police)

Public Order Training

Martin Phillips & Me, 1990

Return to Greyfriars Police Station, 1990
(By kind permission of Bedfordshire Police)

Inspector with section on Drugs Raid

Senior Officers at Greyfriars Police Station, circa 1990
(By kind permission of Bedfordshire police)

Inspector with HQ Training Dept.
(By kind permission of Bedfordshire police)

Training Inspector

BSc (Hons) Degree

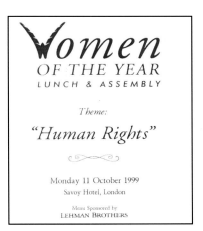

Invitation to Women of the Year Luncheon, 1999

Chief Carole's top honour

CAROLE Phillips joined the police force 27 years ago because she wanted to be a beat bobby.

Last December she became Chief Inspector and on Monday will be one of 500 high-achieving ladies at a prestigious Women of the Year lunch at the Savoy.

Carole, from Biggleswade, is Bedfordshire's first female force training officer, in charge of training its 1600 staff.

"Initially I didn't have career aspirations," said Carole, 49, "but then as my aspirations have changed so has the force, and I have learned how to sell myself."

When she joined female officers had to specialise in work involving women and children - whether they wanted to or not.

It's all changed now though: "Women are on-

couraged to go for promotion now. We're very much part of the team working with our male colleagues," she said. Today, three of the county's 13 chief inspectors are women.

Carole, who left a librarianship for a less predictable line of work, certainly found one with Bedfordshire Police.

Knife

"The most satisfying was community work I have done in Biggleswade," she said.

"The most exciting was surveillance work, and the most dangerous was when someone came at me with a carving knife."

Of Monday's illustrious lunch date, she said: "I have been fortunate to enjoy a challenging but rewarding career and I am looking forward to this opportunity of meeting other women with a wide range of in-

teresting experiences."

But in today's climate of equal opportunity in the police Carole insists: "I never see myself as a woman police officer; I very much regard my-

● **Carole Phillips**

self as a member of a team in the police service."

Chief Inspector Alison Macho, from Leighton Buzzard, has also been invited.

Women of Year, 1999
(By kind permission of the Bedford Times & Citizen)

139

Promoted to Superintendent, January 1999

Superintendent arrives in Pink Office

Superintendent at Biggleswade Remembrance Day Parade
(Photo by kind permission of the Biggleswade Chronicle)

National Firearms Silver Commanders Course 2/99
17th May - 21st May 1999

Back Row: Supt Liz Coulson(Beds), Supt Carole Phillips(Beds), C/I Nick Reeves(Sussex), C/I Steve O'Rourke(Sussex), Supt Jerry Allard(Beds), C/I Mike Flynn(Sussex), C/I Andy Denton(D&C), Supt Phil Davies(D&C).
Front Row: Supt Andy Clarke(D&C), D/Supt John Langley(Derby), Inspector Dick Baker, Sgt John Clingell, D/Supt Kelvin Ashby(Derby), C/I Ian Hobbs(Wilts).

Firearms Course at Exeter

Enjoying painting in retirement, 2003

With husband Martin playing golf in retirement, 2002

Retired police officers (NARPO) reunion at Greyfriars
Police Station, checking out the old cells
(Photo by kind permission of George L. Spurling)

NARPO visit to Greyfriars Police Station, feeling at home
in my old office
(Photo by kind permission of George L Spurling)

Invited to Bedfordshire Police HQ, 2015
(Photo by kind permission of Bedfordshire Police)

Police HQ June 2015, 100 years of women in policing
(Photo by kind permission of Bedfordshire Police)

Police HQ June 2015, Lecture Theatre naming ceremony
(Photo by kind permission of Bedfordshire Police)

Carole & Joan Deja Vu – back at Greyfriars Police
Station, 2015
(By kind permission of ITV Broadcasting)

(Carole meets Eileen Normington (aged 98) Plymouth's 1st policewoman in 1939

Three generations of Bedfordshire Policewomen, PC Katherine Hardy, Inspector Annita Clarke & retired Superintendent Carole Phillips – 2015

(By kind permission of ITV Broadcasting)

Chapter 9

Police Home Defence Duties

In addition to supervising a section of patrol officers, divisional Sergeants had a range of other extraneous duties to meet national or local requirements. In the 1970s and 1980s, Britain was still in the 'Cold War' and the threat of nuclear attack from the USSR was still a real possibility. If there were an attack, police officers would have a role to inform, organise and control the general public. At Greyfriars, one of our Inspectors was nominated as Home Defence Training Officer and regularly ensured that we were aware of the latest guidance from the Home Office. The War Duties Manual was kept locked in the front office safe with other emergency planning documents and in the event of a nuclear attack, would be taken out and utilised by the senior officer on duty.

Police duties included maintaining internal security and preventing sabotage or subversion, guarding key points and prohibited areas such as Government installations and fuel distribution points. We would also escort priority personnel such as dignitaries and senior police, fire and NHS staff to secret bunkers. They would form the Regional Emergency Committee (REC), which would organise and control the county during the interim period and later become part of a national network.

In addition to learning our war duties, Inspectors and Sergeants were made aware of the practical arrangements already in place. Sirens were situated at strategic points in the county and would be activated when information was received from a central point to give members of the public warning to take cover. One such siren was located on the roof of Greyfriars Police Station.

In the police station front office there was a small grey box on the wall with a receiver, a telephone handset, a loud speaker and on/off switch. The telephone was connected to the Ballistic Missile Early Warning System (BMEWS) which was an intelligence sharing system between the UK and USA. One of the radar detector bases for BMEWS was RAF Fylingdales on the North Yorkshire Moors. Most people knew that it was part of the Cold War four minute warning system

When the police station unit was switched on, it emitted a low peeping sound. If a nuclear attack was imminent the device would be turned on by the Station Sergeant and then monitored. If the peeping sound changed to a constant wailing noise, you had only a matter of minutes to take cover.

All officers received Home Defence Training and were advised of their specific duties should an attack occur. We learned about nuclear explosions, Ground Zero and subsequent shock waves. If you didn't die immediately, you would then start to worry about radiation because following an attack, particles called Roentgens would be blown in the wind, pollute the atmosphere and cause radiation sickness. We would be exposed, as we were responsible for patrol and reconnaissance immediately after an attack, to determine the extent of damage and radiation.

If we survived the exposure to radiation, we would then assist with marshalling the homeless, control of essential service routes and controlling the public in fallout zones to maintain order and prevent rioting and looting.

I had a sneaking suspicion that quite a few officers would fail to turn up for duty, as they would choose to protect their own loved ones in those last few hours, but these were not opinions to be publicly voiced.

Every police officer would be issued with a personal dosimeter, which was about the size of a chubby pen and would be clipped to the uniform lapel. We were each to monitor our personal dosimeter, especially if on outside duties. There was an acceptable level of radiation when we would be expected to carry on with our public duties, but when critical level was reached you knew that you would almost certainly die from radiation sickness.

Police humour meant that there was always much speculation as to what each of us would actually do if the station device started to wail, informing us that we only had four minutes to live. Suggestions included boiling an egg, making a cup of tea or phoning the family, but inevitably with so many young men, sexual fantasies were paramount. As only one in ten officers were women, from what I heard, it seemed that we could be very busy meeting demands in those four minutes!

We all had our doubts that all this planning would actually save anyone in the event of a nuclear war. It seemed obvious that Government priority would be to maintain executive power at national level and there never could be a plan to save ordinary members of the public.

The Inspector in charge of Home Defence Training delegated a specific task to me. In addition to the personal dosimeters, the Division held a Roentgen meter, which was a larger and more sophisticated piece of kit for measuring radioactive fallout. He put me in charge of the Roentgen meter, which is a type of Geiger counter. It was a heavy oblong shape, about one foot long, with a yellow plasticised exterior and several dials on the upper surface. I would be responsible for checking overall radiation levels at the police station. The Roentgen meter was kept in my locker in the Sergeant's office and I was to test it regularly to ensure that a red light illuminated when turned on. I was on night duty when I carried out the routine test. The red light illuminated, but all the other dials remained static and presumably would remain so, unless there was nuclear fallout. It occurred to me that there should be a way of testing that the equipment actually worked. This logical approach led to me doing one of the most stupid things in my police career.

Domestic microwaves were still fairly new to British homes and I was the proud owner of one. I had read that it was important to have them checked regularly as there could be some radiation seepage around the door. I now had chance to 'kill two birds with one stone' by checking out the Roentgen meter and my microwave, so at the end of the nightshift I took the meter home with me. My family were in bed when I got home at 6.30am and I usually stayed up to make breakfast for my husband and daughter and see them off to work and school. I put the kettle on to make tea and then put a bowl of water in the microwave and set the timer for a few minutes. I turned on the device and waved the Roentgen meter around the microwave door. There wasn't the slightest flicker on the dials, so I began to doubt the efficacy of the device. Not wanting to be in charge of a useless piece of kit, I decided to test it further. Maybe it was the tiredness after a night shift, misplaced female logic or downright stupidity, but I stood the device in the microwave, set it for ten seconds and shut the door. There was an almighty bang, the dials of the Roentgen meter turned black and the whole device looked like it had been in a war zone. Reality dawned on me, just as my husband came rushing downstairs and I was left to explain what had happened. He just couldn't believe what I had done and couldn't offer any reassurance when it came to the trouble I would be in at work.

I carried out my domestic duties as normal and then tried to get some sleep, but needless to say there were to be no sweet dreams that day. I was back on duty at 10 pm that evening, but went in at 6 pm to see the Inspector responsible for War Duties. I tried to prepare him by saying, "I'm afraid Sir that I have been particularly stupid in relation to looking after the Roentgen meter", I then told him what had happened and hung my head in shame. He looked shocked, told me that the Roentgen meter was a very expensive piece of kit and that he would have to refer the matter to the Superintendent. I had to submit a detailed report and was advised that there could be discipline proceedings for misuse of police property.

I worked the following two night shifts, only telling my section Inspector what had happened, because I felt that I would be a laughing stock if my male colleagues heard what I had done.

I am quite sure that my senior officers must have been incredulous and had a good laugh at my expense, because two days later I was advised that a replacement Roentgen meter had been ordered and that no action would be taken against me. I remained responsible for the equipment and fortunately never got to know if it would work following a nuclear blast!

Chapter 10

Silence in Court

During the 1970's and 1980s, Bedfordshire Police, in common with most other Police Forces, prosecuted its own traffic offences and simple criminal cases at Magistrates Court, there being no Crown Prosecution Service or other independent body.

Both as a Constable and as a Patrol Sergeant at Greyfriars Police Station, I had often visited the Prosecutions Department. My purpose had been to liaise with the Sergeant in that department to ensure that my own cases, or those of my constables, were progressing satisfactorily. Although decisions to prosecute, caution or take no action were made by an Inspector and verified by the Superintendent, the Sergeant was responsible for thoroughly reviewing every file and ensuring that the prosecution case had been fully investigated. He would consider the points to prove and any legal loopholes, alibis or possible mitigation, if necessary calling for further enquiries to be undertaken. He would fully prepare the case for court, fix a date for the hearing and then be available to prosecute. It was only the very complex cases, or those for Quarter Sessions (now known as Crown Courts), which were put out to solicitors or barristers.

Whenever I entered the Sergeant's office in the Prosecution Department, I would thank my lucky stars that I was not doing his job. I loved the outdoor life, the challenge and excitement of patrol work. By contrast, my colleague always seemed buried in paperwork. Every day the clerks heaped his desk with piles of files in brown manila folders that had arrived from the sections and been marked up for prosecution by the Prosecutions Inspector and Superintendent. Unfortunately, the buck stopped with the Sergeant, both in the final preparation and at court. Each pile represented the court list for one day and file preparation commenced two or three weeks ahead of the scheduled court date. At busy times, the Sergeant's desk looked rather like the New York skyline and when the desk was full, the clerks just made new piles on the windowsills. This seemed to cut out the light and I noticed that Sergeants in this post usually looked pale, older than their true age and wore spectacles with heavy lenses. I assumed that this post was normally allocated to Sergeants who were past their sell-by-date for patrol duties, and who were eagerly awaiting retirement. In my view, the Sergeant's only excitement came when he dusted off his best uniform and attended the Magistrates Court. Here he would sit for hours, alongside defence solicitors, on a hard wooden bench, only leaping up to speak whenever protocol demanded.

My only experience of Magistrates Court was when I was required to attend to give evidence in specific cases. This usually involved a long wait in the draughty main hall of Shire Hall Magistrates Court, St .Paul's Square, Bedford. This very impressive, lofty building had the kind of traditional, rather Gothic architecture, which seemed to be able to put the fear of God into defendants, witnesses and young police officers alike. The five courtrooms were also of rather grand proportions with imposing high wooden benches for the magistrate and court officials. On court days, remand prisoners were transferred from Greyfriars

Police Station, Bedford, to the Victorian style cells under the courts. When their case was called, they would be handcuffed and escorted by a constable up the stone staircase into the isolated 'dock'. Here, they were fully on view to all gathered in the courtroom and public gallery. Witnesses, when called, took a long, lonely walk across the courtroom to the witness stand, where they could often be seen visibly shaking as they took the oath.

As young police officers' we received some training at police training school on how to give evidence. It was important to look confident, speak clearly and present a professional image. Most defence solicitors would try to discredit police evidence, or that of other witnesses, so one did not expect an easy ride. Giving evidence was an essential part of policing, so I was pleased to discover that it was an area where I seemed to acquit myself rather well. As a young probationer-constable I had received a commendation from the magistrates for the manner in which I had presented my evidence in a complex burglary case. This seemed to give me the confidence that I needed and as I gained experience in both Magistrates' Court and Crown Court I even began to enjoy the cut and thrust of being cross-examined. I was, nonetheless, usually very pleased to resume patrol duties away from the stifling atmosphere of the court. I could not imagine myself ever wanting to spend much time in the confines of the court, so for a number of reasons, the job of Sergeant in the Prosecutions Department was definitely not for me.

At the time of annual appraisals, I enthusiastically outlined my personal career aspirations to my senior officers, who nodded appreciatively. It came as a shock therefore in January 1977, when the Superintendent informed me that a vacancy had arisen for a Sergeant in the prosecutions department and I had been selected for the post. In those disciplined days, I accepted that, as a divisional officer, I was deployed on any duties that the boss felt appropriate and I did not even consider arguing my case. I did tell him that I was particularly happy as a Patrol Sergeant and felt that I ran a good team. He replied, "I know that you will be missed by your section, but I am sure you will do an excellent job in Prosecutions. You will start on Monday".

My patrol-section were also surprised by my posting, but they still managed to give me a superb leaving do. Following a late shift, the whole section went up to the bar and social area on the fourth floor of the police station and we partied in the traditional way. During the farewell speeches, I was given many accolades for being a good leader and teased mercilessly about my feminine charms and my ability to put the fear of God into some of the men. They presented me with a lipstick and a lovely compact engraved with the Force crest. Apparently, they had noticed that I liked to retouch my lipstick before I went to a confrontation or fight. They were right, applying 'war – paint' gave me extra confidence and made me feel in control of the situation, even if I did end up in a punch up.

I was to use and treasure that compact for many years to come. Meanwhile, my section officers seemed to be suitably touched when, for the first time, they saw me lost for words and with tears in my eyes. They were a superb team and I was very sad to be leaving them, even if I was to be working in the same building.

The following Monday, I reported to the Inspector in charge of prosecutions. He explained that my predecessor who was on sick leave, intended to retire. The Inspector had checked the files for court that day. These were mainly 'guilty plea traffic cases', but there would also be the usual liquor licensing applications for 'protection orders' or 'extensions'. This was an area that I knew little about, but I nodded intelligently. The Inspector explained the court procedures and said that I had an hour to read the files before we attended court. He would come with me, demonstrate procedures, watch me present a few cases and then leave to attend to other duties. This type of 'on the job training' was fairly common in the police service at that time, so I was not surprised to have to 'hit the ground running'. Regardless of having given evidence, the court-room was still rather an alien environment to me and I did feel rather anxious about making a fool of myself in public.

As I read the files, I realised that for many of the cases, as soon as a guilty-plea was entered by the defendant or his solicitor, all I would have to do was read out a statement of facts and an antecedent history of the defendant, ask for costs and leave the rest to the magistrate. That did not seem too bad, but each file had notes on the front, written in what seemed to be hieroglyphics to me. Every police department had its' own terminology and abbreviations and this one was no exception. The Inspector gave me a brief explanation, as we brushed down our best uniforms, donned our hats and strode purposefully across town to the court building. We both carried enormous brown leather brief cases and I was aware that I had a busy day ahead. I certainly had no time to be bored in my new role. My mind was whirring with all the procedures and protocols that had been explained to me.

On arrival at the court building, we walked up the stone steps to the main foyer, passing many of the nervous defendants having their last cigarette, before entering the building. I realised that if I was nervous, so were they, and they had no idea that I was new to the role. The court usher acknowledged us with a deferent nod of his head. We then entered the courtroom and took our seats on the prosecution bench. Although the prosecutor remained in court throughout the court sitting, there would be a flurry of comings and goings as solicitors checked the listings and usually slid into their place just before their client was summoned to the dock. It seemed that, even before the Inspector and I had taken the files from our brief cases, solicitors involved in licensing applications, defence lawyers and members of the local press approached us. Everyone had questions, wanted to discuss plea-bargaining or, in the case of the press, wanted to know about any interesting cases with a good storyline. This was a hectic time and I soon realised just how prepared the prosecutor needed to be before setting foot into the court building. Perhaps there was a lot more to this job than I had imagined.

When the magistrates entered the court, we all stood and, following the Inspector's lead, I bowed my head to the magistrates in the same way as all the legal representatives. The chairman of the bench acknowledged and then we all took our seats. The Inspector introduced me to the bench of magistrates as 'the new prosecutor' and then the work of the court began. I hoped that no one would realise just how nervous I felt. The licensing cases were dispensed with in a speedy manner and then the Inspector presented a number of traffic cases. He then handed all the files to me and as the next case was called I rose to my feet. I heard my own voice coming across loud and clear as I presented facts and antecedents, asked for costs and then thanked the magistrates. There were a few 'not guilty pleas' and I enjoyed calling the witnesses and eliciting the evidence from them. When a defendant gave evidence on his own behalf or called witnesses I enjoyed the challenge of asking testing questions, sometimes to rebut what seemed to be obvious lies. Occasionally, a defence solicitor would object to a particular line of questions and I would defer, but only because I needed to do some extra research on the rules of evidence. During a short adjournment by the bench of magistrates, my Inspector said, "You're doing a grand job kid. I'll leave you to it and see you back at Greyfriars later." As he left, I realised that my nerves had dissipated and I felt rather empowered to be in such a high profile job. The rest of the court session seemed to go amazingly quickly and I felt a sense of achievement as the huge heap of files moved from one side of the bench to the other. I had neatly recorded all the results, but not necessarily in the usual abbreviated form. I would sort out the hieroglyphics later.

As the court ended and the magistrates rose to retire, the chairman of the bench said, "Thank you Sergeant. You did an excellent job." I acknowledged by bowing my head and saying "Thank you sir". It may have been appropriate to appear very cool, but I was delighted and gave the magistrates a beaming smile. After the court ended, I packed away the files, had a brief discussion with some of the solicitors and then left. As I walked back to the police station I reflected upon the day and realised that, regardless of my initial feelings, this job, or at least the court proceedings, were something that I might come to enjoy.

The office work now took on a new importance, as I checked files and considered every possible line of questioning or defence. I remembered what it was like to be a Constable or Sergeant on night shift completing paperwork. The arrest had always seemed like a good idea but at 5 o'clock in the morning, when the brain was crying out for sleep, it was sometimes difficult to be an efficient report writer. I worked closely with the section officers ensuring that their files were of the highest possible standards and that every possible avenue of investigation had been pursued. On occasions, it became clear that there was a significant weakness in the prosecution case and I arranged to have the prosecution withdrawn. This was not only fair to the defendant, but saved embarrassment for the police and the potential award of costs against us. In addition to informing the defendant, I always took the time to explain to the officer in the case exactly why such action had been taken. I began to comprehend that the role of Prosecuting Sergeant was very much part of the big team. I also began to appreciate the amount of essential work carried out by the clerks and typists working in the department. I had not previously worked closely with civilian staff, but now, in order to be an effective manager, I found myself having to learn a great deal about the different working regulations. I soon realised that, whereas a uniformed section was run on discipline and respect, there was a different management style required in a support office environment. All the civilian staff were female and I found it much easier than the male Sergeants to enter their world, understand some of their problems, and develop a happy working relationship. The team leader eventually told me that it was good for them to have a boss who really cared and that I could rely on their hard work and full support. This experience would prove to be very useful to me in future years when I gained promotion to higher ranks. It may be the police officers, who do the exciting, more 'sexy' work, but it is the, lesser paid, civilian support staff, who are often responsible for keeping the machinery running and they deserve the support and thanks of their police colleagues.

The enormous heaps of court files stacked around my office now no longer seemed so daunting as I viewed each file as simply another challenge that would come to fruition in court. I began to spend many extra hours researching case law, studying 'Stones Justices Manual'. I tried to ensure that when I arrived in Court, I was well prepared for any eventuality and even had a few tricks up my own sleeve. Once I had 'cut my teeth' on traffic offences, I started to thoroughly enjoy prosecuting crime cases with 'not guilty' pleas. Such cases were a chance to develop my skills of cross-examination and pit my wits against local solicitors, or occasionally a barrister. I soon learned that solicitors were usually reasonably conversant with their clients cases, having met the client on at least one occasion, but sometimes were lacking in their final preparation, having only read the court file that morning. Conversely, highly paid barristers had often been briefed by a solicitor and, at best, only spent a few minutes with the defendant before the court hearing. Consequently, barristers, in my experience, tended to rely on grand, theatrical performances, which sometimes raised an expression of surprise on even the defendant's face! I decided that, if I were ever in trouble with the law, I would much rather choose a local solicitor who knew me rather than a rather grand barrister who might be tempted to play the game at my expense. It seemed to me that local solicitors had their reputation at stake, but barristers often breezed into town, gave over dramatic performances for their own grandiosity and then breezed out again. Such performances seemed more fitting for a television drama than for a 'shoplifting' case in the local court.

During my early days in court, I found the solicitors very friendly, but also quite prepared to take advantage of any lack of knowledge on my part. In my initial address, during cross-examination of a witness, or during 'summing up', I was sometimes distracted by one of their formal objections. Sometimes this appeared to be mere theatrics, as the solicitor concerned 'bobbed up', made some comment which the magistrate rejected, and then sat down again. I soon learned to fully research each case and then have the courage of my own convictions unless the magistrate sustained the objection. I learned to argue my case, quoting where appropriate from the Justices Manual or from other stated cases. I became a competent advocate and fully believed that my role was to elicit the truth, whether that led to a conviction or acquittal. I would agree that, like others in the court, I enjoyed giving a performance, but I hope that I never treated it as a game. I was all too aware that what was simply 'a case' to me was also a traumatic event for the victim and a worrying time for the offender. An individual disqualified from driving could also lose their job. A person convicted of a crime, and sentenced to imprisonment, often lost their livelihood, their home and sometimes their family. Many dramas took place in the courtroom and, although I was required to remain impassive, I was sometimes amazed by the stories of human frailty, wickedness or even ingenuity. In many ways, a court is rather like a theatre, with each person appearing, playing a specific role and wearing appropriate costume for the day. This is particularly the case at the higher level courts where the judge appears in his wig and gown and all the barristers follow suit. It can also be observed that many an arch villain, who gets caught looking the part in his rough 'working clothes', will appear in court wearing a suit and sporting a new smart haircut. Even police officers would wear their best uniform for court. This was particularly the case for female officers, who in the late 1970's, were allowed to wear trousers whilst on night duty, but when called to court, they were expected to arrive wearing a skirt and tunic. It was rather like attending church, as female officers, unlike their male colleagues, were also required to wear their uniform hat whilst in court.

In the Magistrates' Courts, the magistrates themselves tended to set the scene. Some required more 'pomp and circumstance' than others. Magistrates are not legally trained professionals, but are locally selected volunteers from varied walks of life, appointed by the Crown. One of the magistrates, who I could not help admire, had the title of Colonel. He was Chairman of the Bench, a local landowner and lived in a fine manor house in rural Bedfordshire. He had a long association with Bedfordshire Police as a magistrate, as well as having served as a member of the Police Committee and as Lord Lieutenant for the County. I had previously had no contact with anyone from the landed gentry and, consequently, I found him fascinating. In Court, he adhered to the strictest protocols and treated all officials and defendants with fairness and respect. During proceedings, he always referred to me formally as 'Sergeant', but occasionally if he saw me at the end of Court proceedings, when he was much more relaxed he would refer to me as 'my dear' and be very charming. To me, the Colonel was the epitome of the kindly, but strict old granddad of story tales. He was a larger than life character and, despite his elderly years, he still had a military bearing and a very commanding voice. Any one appearing before his court, be they prosecutor, solicitor or defendant, needed to be aware that the Colonel would not stand any nonsense in his court. He particularly disliked someone who gave mitigating circumstances that were based on pure fantasy and only prolonged the work of the court. On the other hand, I found the Colonel to be an absolute gentleman with a sense of fairness developed through experience. He may have always lived a privileged life, but his Army experience had allowed him to witness hardship and he seemed to recognise a needy individual when they appeared before him. Even when sentencing one of the well-known local 'down and outs' for drunkenness, stealing or begging, I suspected that he knew he was at least giving them a warm bed and hot food for a week or two. Such people were a nuisance around the town, but in the absence of proper hostels and treatment centres, there seemed little alternative but to send them to prison. The prisoner's response to such a sentence was often "Thank you kindly, Sir".

On one occasion, in a case of dangerous driving, the Colonel was chairing the magistrates' court alongside two of his magistrate colleagues. The defendant was a businessman who appointed a barrister to defend him. The barrister was from out of town, did not know the Colonel and acted in a very arrogant manner throughout the hearing. I gave the facts of the case, which were quite simple. The defendant had been speeding through town, overtaking everything in his path and generally being aggressive towards other drivers and pedestrians, even to the point of putting lives at risk. The defending barrister did not call his client to give evidence, but proceeded to give a very long speech in mitigation, which used every excuse in the book. He finished by saying that he felt sure that the magistrates would not wish to disqualify his client, who would, consequently, not be able to get to work and support his family. The Colonel, who had looked exceptionally bored throughout the barrister's speech, whispered briefly to his colleagues. He then indicated that the defendant should stand, and then said, "When I was a boy, I learned that wrong-doing had to be paid for. You may have a journey of ten miles to work at inconvenient times, but you should have thought of that earlier. Get yourself a bicycle. You will be disqualified for twelve months." I found it hard not to smile at this kind of straightforward summary justice. It seemed ironic that the defendant, in employing a barrister to present his case, had certainly not improved his chances. Good old-fashioned honesty and a sense of humility would no doubt have served him better.

At that time, there seemed to be few if any female solicitors working in Bedford, so the court was mainly a male environment. I fully admit to thoroughly enjoying lots of attention in my official capacity, as well as quite a lot of sexist teasing from my male colleagues when the court was not sitting. I think they were sometimes surprised at my quick and occasionally rather cheeky responses, developed over the years from working with policemen. When the court-proceedings commenced, we all resumed our professional mantles.

Occasionally, the Police would employ local solicitors to prosecute complex cases or those, which were likely to end up in Crown Court and be passed to barristers. We therefore built up a good working relationship with many of the solicitors and were used to seeing them acting for the prosecution or defence in an impartial manner. This also meant that we would meet on social occasions either at the police station or at local public houses and subsequently get to know each other as individuals.

Several of the solicitors played rugby or cricket and were known socially to members of the police teams having shared a 'few jars' together. As a woman, I was excluded from some of this camaraderie, but the resultant gossip certainly gave me a good idea of some of the real characters.

There were about a dozen local solicitors who frequently attended the court to defend clients. Each had his own specific style of advocacy and one could anticipate the line of defence before he said a word. It was essential that I got to know the solicitors and their specific styles, so that I could ensure that any plea-bargaining that took place was both ethical and appropriate. Sometimes, the prosecutor agreed to drop an offence and accept a guilty plea on a lesser offence. This was usually on the basis that the defence solicitor, and their client, accepted the facts as stated by the prosecution and did not then try to mitigate to gain further advantage. Generally, there was an excellent working relationship amongst all those involved in the court procedures and each day was interesting and challenging.

There was one well-known local solicitor, who added character to the court, but also seemed to make my job very simple. He was a dapper man who always wore a pin-striped suit and a 'signature' rose in the button-hole of his suit jacket. He never seemed to deal with 'not guilty' pleas, but preferred to get his client to plead guilty, thus enabling him to give one of his standard speeches of mitigation. His clients were no doubt impressed by his heart-rending pleas on their behalf, but regular members of the court had all heard the same 'flowery speech' many times. Sometimes he went on a bit too long and both he and his rose appeared badly wilted by the end of proceedings. He did not seem to mind a bit of teasing from his colleagues, being quite content with an easy life and a pay cheque at the end.

Occasionally, a solicitor accepted the case against his client, negotiated a reduction in charges, and then later proceeded to challenge the statement given by me on behalf of the prosecution. Protocol precluded me from responding in open court. On one occasion, when I felt that a solicitor had taken a very unfair advantage, I made it quite clear to him afterwards that, in future, the prosecution would not be open to negotiation with him. He said words to me to the extent that 'all was fair in love and in court'. This was like a red rag to a bull and was the beginning of a number of sparring matches between us. He seemed to be disarmingly charming before court and then use every trick in the book to try to win his case. It was sometimes during the summing-up by the defence that I found him saying things, which were either unfairly criticising the prosecution, or saying things about his client, which I knew to be, at best, 'gilding the lily'. At this stage in proceedings, I had no opportunity to reply. It was on one such occasion that I remembered his words 'all is fair in love and in court' and decided to act, albeit in a rather unprofessional way. I was sitting very close to him as he stood to address the court. Without moving, and behind the high wooden bench, I slipped off my shoe and began to caress his leg with my stockinged foot. I continued to look passively and impartially towards the magistrates, but listened carefully to what the defence solicitor was saying. He soon began to sound rather flustered and cut his speech to a minimum. I quickly replaced my shoe and continued proceedings as if nothing had happened. Strangely enough, neither he nor I ever mentioned what had happened. Maybe he could not believe it and I was simply glad to have got away with my misbehaviour.

During the following week, the same solicitor was again defending a client in a case where I was prosecuting.

I declined to negotiate and was determined to present all the facts and have an opportunity to cross-examine his client if appropriate, or make any relevant objections. I took my time in presenting the facts to the court, enlightening them with every detail of his client's criminal behaviour. I then sat down to await his lengthy response. I was amazed when he looked very uncomfortable, shuffled in his seat, and then stood for a few moments making minimal, but rather high-pitched comment. The court sentenced his client, the case was over very quickly, and the solicitor seemed literally to dash from the court. I wondered if he was a changed man or simply felt ill. I later discovered the truth. The solicitor was a keen sportsman and had been playing rugby on the previous day. He had pulled a muscle in his thigh, so that morning, after showering, he applied a liberal amount of 'Ralgex' to the aching muscle. He had then dressed and hurried to court. On taking his seat on the solicitors' bench, his underpants, which had somehow become smeared with Ralgex, came into contact with delicate parts of his anatomy. His agony was apparently unspeakable, as was his prepared speech to the court! I could not help but smile at what seemed to be natural justice.

There was one occasion when I managed to get the full attention of the court for all the wrong reasons. I was always careful to be immaculately dressed in my best police uniform. My long black hair was coiled into a neat chignon pinned at the back. I probably looked smart, but somewhat prim. Although etiquette at that time was for policewomen to keep their hats on in court, when I was appointed prosecutor and then spent many hours in court, the magistrates gave me a general permission to remove my hat in court. I therefore used to enter the court wearing my police hat, which I then removed and placed on the desk in front of me.

One day whilst off duty I decided to change my hairstyle and colour. I went to a hairdressing salon in town and told them that I wanted to change my hair to a honey blond colour and have it cut short. The hairdresser said that this would not be a problem. After four hours, however, when the salon was due to close, my hair had turned a bright orange colour and looked rather spiky. I was given a bottle of ash blond solution to keep applying and assured that I would eventually reach the desired colour. I did not have to pay, although the hairdressers all told me that the colour was really 'quite nice' and would look different away from the fluorescent lights of the shop!

The following morning I stood looking at my hair in the bathroom mirror. After many applications of the prescribed product, my hair was still rather a vivid orange colour, so I was glad to be able to twist it into a bun and pile it under my uniform hat ready for duty. I arrived in court, calmly took my seat, placed all my files on the desk and awaited the arrival of the magistrates. When they arrived, the Chairman of the Bench said to me "Sergeant it's a very warm day, so do feel free to remove your hat" I declined, but he kindly insisted, so I complied. There was a discernible gasp from all assembled in the court, but no one said a word. My bright pinkish-orange mop tumbled from under my hat and left everyone speechless. I then carried on with my work of prosecuting in the normal way, but was very much aware that I had the full attention of the court throughout.

Life in court and in the prosecution office was far from boring and I began to appreciate the words of my Superintendent when he gave me the job and said, "the experience will be good for you". In this role I gained in confidence, acquired a flair for public speaking, and greatly enhanced my legal knowledge. For the first time in my police service, I was working regular office hours, so I also appreciated the rest and recuperation from shift work. I remained in the post for two years and when my next posting came, I was reluctant to move on.

Chapter 11

Mum's the Word

I enjoyed all the variety of life as a Sergeant and was always keen to develop my career. Once again, I studied hard and in 1980 passed the promotion exam to Inspector. I then attended a promotion board and received notification that I would be promoted when a vacancy arose.

I now felt that I had a clear career plan and my husband, now also promoted to Sergeant, supported my aspirations. We had tried for a family, but it hadn't worked out, so it seemed that nothing was in my way. Nature, however, sometimes has the final say and within months I found that I was pregnant. I suffered badly from morning sickness, but managed to keep the news secret for four months, hoping that I would be promoted before making my announcement. The promotion didn't happen and my uniform was getting too tight, so I put in a report advising my senior officers of the situation. I stated that I would take maternity leave and if my child was fit and well, I would return to work.

Other policewomen who had previously had children had left the Police, so there were no laid down procedures for work during maternity or for return to work. I continued to work full time until I was seven months pregnant. There were no special arrangements, so I ordered a bigger uniform and just carried on with my normal duties, including arresting shoplifters. The design of our uniforms with a box jacket was ideal as it hid the bump very well. An Inspector's vacancy arose on the division, but I was not promoted as my senior officers just assumed that I would soon leave the Force.

When I went on maternity leave, I enjoyed the rest and happily prepared for my baby, but I did feel very cut off from the job that had been my life for twelve years. I knew that if all went well I would want to return to my job in the police service.

My daughter Michelle was born in May 1981 and I returned to work six months later. Although my childcare arrangements were very good, my Chief Constable, Mr Dyer, said that it was not appropriate to promote a mother with a young child. He was a real gentleman, but had old fashioned, traditional views about family and childcare and could not be persuaded otherwise.

My husband worked shifts and we also had a child minder and help from two granddads, so life soon settled down to a regular pattern. I combined life as a mother and as a Sergeant, which was fulfilling, but exhausting at times, especially when I had sleepless nights. I had to work full time, as there were no part time options, but the Chief Constable did post me to the Social Enquiry and Juvenile Liaison Office (JLO), which enabled me to work day shifts.

The JLO team was made up of male and female uniformed officers and we covered every school in North Bedfordshire from the smallest village primary school, to the largest of the Upper Schools, including the private schools.

One of the most enjoyable parts of the job, was being invited into schools to give talks or show crime prevention films to the pupils. One film that we showed to younger children was 'Stranger Danger', but it had been shown so many times that the film was in poor condition and would sometimes break as it ran through the projector. There would be a gasp of disappointment from the children and some hurried splicing and sticky tape application by one of us. It was very rewarding when the projector started again and there would be a cheer from the children. I don't think the film was that good, but the children were worried about having to go back to their normal classes instead of enjoying something more relaxing. As I now had a child of my own, I began to enjoy working with children and understanding their needs. It was fun entertaining them and building up a rapport. Police hats, truncheons and handcuffs were always popular visual aids and sometimes, I would arrange for a traffic car or dog handler to come along. The aim was to provide safety information and break down barriers to ensure that the children could approach a police officer if they needed help or support. As well as showing the friendly face of the police, we also let the children know that we would be firm and apply the law if they committed a crime or were a public nuisance. As a team, we built up good relationships with school head teachers, who would contact our department if they suspected that a crime was being committed against a pupil (e.g. child abuse or supply of drugs) or if they suspected that a pupil had committed an offence. Our investigation usually culminated in a formal warning or caution, but at least the children involved realised that they couldn't get away with crime.

One day, I received a call from the headmaster of one of the private schools, asking me to visit as there was a problem. It was soon revealed that forty pupils had been away on a three-day school trip to the Cotswolds, visiting all the places of interest. They had pocket money to spend, so were allowed to visit shops in towns and villages. On the bus home, a teacher had noticed a child giving away sweets, pens and pencils from his school bag. She demanded an explanation and eventually the boy admitted stealing the items. The teacher stopped the bus, made an announcement and demanded that if any other children had any stolen items, or had received any, they were to bring them to the front of the bus immediately. She got more than she had bargained for!

In the headmaster's office, I was astounded to see a mountainous heap of sweets, pens, rubbers, jewellery, rubber balls and assorted knick-knacks. Apparently, every child had either stolen something from a shop or subsequently received stolen items.

It would have been easy to address the entire group of pupils and warn them about their behaviour, but I needed to establish who the ringleaders were and whether or not there had been any bullying. Children also should not be interviewed without their parents, so the only way was to interview each child separately. With the headmaster's co-operation, I drew up a schedule of appointments and parents were invited to attend. I also contacted the shops concerned and got agreement not to prosecute. Over the course of two days, together with a PC from JLO, I interviewed all the children and established who stole what, where and when. There were lots of tears from children and some very shocked parents, who were appalled that the police were involved. The final resolution was by way of informal cautions, which meant that none of the children would have a criminal record, but they had all learned a salutary lesson. I was convinced that this zero tolerance to even a minor crime was the right way to tackle the issue and was appreciative that the headmaster trusted the police to take appropriate action.

Shopkeepers who caught young thieves or suspected school children of theft, would often inform our department. I received a complaint about a thirteen-year old girl who had previously been warned by a shopkeeper for stealing from his shop, but who was now suspected of stealing small items on a regular basis. There was no conclusive evidence, but I agreed to speak to her and her parent. I visited her home and knocked on the door. The girl opened the door and I asked her to get her mother, but she responded with a string of expletives and then tried to slam the door in my face. I had half anticipated this, so speedily put my foot in the door and then called for her mother. She came, but would not let me inside, so we had a conversation on the doorstep. I explained the circumstances and as there was insufficient evidence to arrest, I gave the girl advice, hoping to keep her out of future trouble. The girl was still stroppy and used foul language, so before I left I told her that if she ever used language like that to a police officer again, she would get a 'clip round the ear'. I said to the mother, "I'm sure you agree" but she made no comment.

Back at the police station, the Inspector told me that the girl's mother had phoned in to complain about my conduct. I was subsequently interviewed by the Discipline and Complaints Department and admitted what had happened. In due course, I was given a formal warning by the Chief Superintendent about my 'Oppressive Conduct'. As I left his office, he called, "By the way Sergeant, carry on the good work!"

I found it interesting that all the stories about a good old-time Copper, related to how he wouldn't stand any nonsense and would give a stroppy youth a 'clip around the ear'. The rhetoric was sound, but in practice it would have to be administered away from the public eye, as it seemed society would not back the officer who got caught.

The JLO also dealt with child abuse; receiving information from playgroups, schools or hospitals when a child was acting strangely or marks were seen on their bodies. I dealt with some heart-rending cases, including 'grooming' and sexual abuse of borders at a private school.

The children were so vulnerable and had nobody to turn to as most of their parents were living abroad. When the matter came to light, my JLO team of six officers had to interview around forty children, many of whom did not have English as their first language. This was harrowing and very sensitive work. The headmaster was eventually convicted of a range of sexual offences, but many of those children were likely to be permanently damaged. Sometimes, children would be taken into immediate care, but usually, a JLO officer would attend a case conference with Social Services and other agencies to decide on the way forward. This was important work, but physically and mentally draining. It was one aspect of police work that could leave me feeling tearful and often kept me awake at night.

It was at these times that I really appreciated having a loving family to go home to, Simple things like reading my daughter a bedtime story and giving her a 'Good night' kiss helped me to keep my belief in human nature. I kept my favourite photo of my daughter on my desk to remind me of the important precious things in life.

I kept applying for promotion, but still got turned down by my Chief Constable. When I went before another promotion board, the Chief Constable said that he thought that I should be at home looking after my baby and that 'working mothers were the cause of latch key children and problems in society'. He did however state that he had read the favourable reports from my divisional senior officers and agreed that my professional competence was not in doubt.

I was more frustrated than angry, especially as there was no procedure for appeal against his decision. I spoke to my representative in the Police Federation, but it became obvious that, as mine was a 'one off case', there was no political will to pursue the matter.

The British Association for Women in Policing (BAWP) was not founded until 1987, so there was no 'Gender Agenda' or recognised good practice for maternity leave and subsequent promotion.

It was clear that either I accepted the situation with good grace and continued to work hard, or I would have to leave the Police Force. I decided to stay and develop other career options.

Chapter 12

Reaching New Depths

After a year working as Sergeant in charge of the Juvenile Liaison Department (JLO), I had convinced myself, my husband and most of my senior officers, that I could successfully combine my police career with being a wife and mother. I was working regular hours and life seemed quite comfortable. Many people, including my husband, told me how lucky I was that things had worked out so well for me and expected me to be very content with my lot in life. I did feel fortunate, but I also felt that my achievement had been as a result of hard work and determination. I had gone through a great deal of soul searching and in the face of some opposition it had been sheer 'bloody mindedness' that had sometimes carried me through. My role in JLO, dealing with offences involving young people and tracing missing persons, was valuable work, but it lacked the challenge and excitement of twenty-four-hour patrol work. Nonetheless, I might have settled for the easy life had it not have been for a job advertisement that I saw in 'Force Orders', the weekly bulletin of promotions, discipline matters, vacancies and logistics. The item that caught my attention was 'Volunteers wanted for the Bedfordshire Police Search and Recovery Team. Selected individuals will train one day per week as police divers and then continue in their regular posts, being available for call-out when necessary'. I felt excited and knew that this was the challenge I was waiting for. I had worked alongside the diving team on many occasions when I had enlisted their help during missing person enquiries, so I had a good understanding of their role.

The following day I typed out my application form, ready to be submitted to Headquarters via my Divisional Commander. I had consulted my husband, who was against the idea and could not understand my wish to take on a new challenge, especially one with associated risks. I told him that this was something that I really wanted to do and that if I did not at least apply and go through the selection process I would never know what opportunities existed. He agreed, on the basis that he did not think that the selectors would choose a woman in any case. This made me more determined and I submitted my application with a real sense of purpose. Within a day, I was summoned to the Chief Superintendent's office. He had previously worked with the diving team and now made it quite clear to me that he would not support my application. He did not think that a woman would fit into the team, mainly because of the logistics of changing into diving gear at remote locations. He also reminded me that, as a wife and mother, my current role was well suited to my family needs. He suggested that I 'be sensible and withdraw this application' and that I should 'put family first, at least for a few years' This was all said in a kindly manner, which had the desired effect of making me feel really guilty for having applied. He then held up my application and said, "In your own interests and in the interest of the job shall we just forget this here and now". I nodded in agreement and my application disappeared into the waste bin, which in the police service was euphemistically knows as 'File 13'. I had given up a dream, but realised that this seemed a necessary compromise to keep my boss and my husband happy. I did not, however, give up the idea of looking for a new challenge.

An opportunity arose later in 1982. One of the diving section members was also a local beat officer. He had become overwhelmed with paperwork and omitted to submit a number of important crime files. With the help of my contacts in the prosecution office, I helped him to sort the situation out without resorting to discipline procedures. He was grateful and said, "If ever I can do you a favour, please let me know." Half-jokingly, I told him about my application to join the Diving Section and said that I would love to have just one dive with the team. He promised to make some enquiries with the team leader. Within a few days, my colleague rang me at Greyfriars Police Station and said, "I have had a discussion with team members and it is agreed that you can dive with us. Monday is a training day at the Blue Lagoon, so if you can get time off, bring your swimming things and meet us at the dive store. Whatever you do, don't let the Chief Super find out." I thanked him and said that I would be there.

I knew that the expanse of water, known locally as the Blue Lagoon, was a deep flooded disused clay pit at Arlesey, Bedfordshire. It was named Blue Lagoon as on sunny days, the greyish white colour of the clay in the base of the pit reflected the light from above. As a result the water often looked an iridescent blue colour of almost Mediterranean appearance. Although this was private water, occasionally used by sailing enthusiasts, local people from the nearby town of Arlesey would trespass in the summer months to swim in the lake. They climbed over the security fences and ignored the notices, so that they could enjoy the pleasures of open water swimming. Unfortunately, swimmers were occasionally taken by surprise by the depth and icy temperatures of the water and several fatalities had occurred. Also situated nearby was Fairfield mental hospital and the lake seemed to have a fatal attraction for some of the depressed patients. This history meant that Bedfordshire Police Diving Section was frequently called upon to search the Blue Lagoon to recover bodies or motor vehicles that had been dumped there. The landowner agreed to allow the Diving team regular access to use the Blue Lagoon for their training sessions,

The following Monday dawned as a bleak, grey March day, but nothing could diminish my excitement. I met the team at the dive store, which was based in the old police cells at Kempston Police Station. We loaded all the equipment into the purpose built dive van and put the rigid inflatable boat onto the trailer. Eight of us then set off for the Blue Lagoon. On arrival at the lakeside, I noted that the water was anything but blue. It looked steely grey and foreboding as it reflected the colour of the dismal grey sky. I was undeterred but did hope that we might catch a glimpse of the sun as the day progressed.

The team immediately went into action brewing hot drinks, preparing and launching the dive boat and filling the air cylinders from the mobile compressor. As I helped to carry gear to the water's edge, the team leader came over and said, "For safety reasons it will be necessary for you to undertake the Royal Life Saving Society (RLSS) Open Water Rescue Bronze Cross Award before you dive with us. One of our team is an official RLSS examiner so if you get changed you can do the test straight away. This seemed perfectly reasonable, as I was a strong swimmer, so within minutes, I changed into my swimsuit and approached the water's edge. My assessor had a clipboard and stopwatch and gave me clear instructions. I was expected to swim fifty yards across the lake to a given point. Then during the return trip I was to find a struggling man on the surface of the water, tow him to safety and place him in the recovery position. The task must be completed in a set time. I was already feeling the cold, but with members of the team watching, I had no intention of showing any weakness. The stopwatch was set and I strode into the freezing water and then launched myself into a swim, using crawl. I was initially taken aback by the intense cold, which took my breath away, but I eventually found a steady pace and let determination take over. My muscles were aching with the cold and my breathing felt shallow, but eventually I reached a buoy in the water and began the return journey. I could see a man in a diving suit in the water and he was feigning distress. I swam around him, pulled him onto his back and took the approved towing hold. My hands were so cold that it was difficult to maintain a grip and as I spoke to try and reassure him I realised that my teeth were chattering so much that I was inaudible. I began to tow him towards the shore and occasionally, I was aware of him moving his legs to help propel us along. I was really struggling when I heard him say "Keep going girl. Don't let it beat you. You are nearly there". This encouragement was just enough to spur me on and eventually I reached shallow water, dragged him onto the shingle beach, placed him in the recovery position and collapsed alongside him. When I eventually stood up, I was blue with cold and covered in goose pimples and must have looked a total wreck. Suddenly, I became aware of clapping and laughter from my new colleagues. I was offered a warm towel and a hot drink. One of the team said, "Well done. Sorry we forgot to tell you that in these conditions you were allowed to wear a dive suit for the test. I didn't know whether to laugh or cry, but guessed that I had just passed the team initiation test, so decided to laugh.

On returning to the dive van, I was given a mug of steaming hot Oxo with a liberal sprinkling of freshly ground black pepper. Within minutes, I could feel the blood coursing around my body and I began to glow. Once I was dressed, I felt as warm as toast and ready for my next challenge.

Within an hour I was fully briefed and ready for a dive. The team leader explained that the team members nearly always dived in dry suits, which were warmer and provided greater protection against pollutants in the local rivers, canals and lakes. Each member of the team had several suits made to measure. I am five feet seven inches tall and had to borrow the suit of a five feet ten inch male, so it was never going to be a good fit!

I watched my diving buddy get into his suit and was astounded that the only way in was through the neck opening. Two colleagues stretched the neck open while the diver wriggled in, getting his feet into the integral boots and then wriggling and pulling the suit up around him. If ever there was a moment when I might have changed my mind this was it! As our helpers brought over my suit I could feel my face going red with embarrassment. They pulled open the neck and one said, "Come on Carole, let's get you in" It was rather like being pushed into an ill-fitting corset, but eventually we got there. My feet were into size nine boots, the suit was tight across my chest and hips, but baggy around the neck, shoulders and legs. I was then fitted with a weight belt, air cylinder and a pair of enormous fins. Next came the metal neck seal and then the helmet and integral face-mask were fitted.

Then, carrying my fins, I waddled down to the boat, climbed aboard and sat on the inflatable side-wall alongside my buddy. The boat was then taken to the middle of the Blue Lagoon and anchored. I was given a last minute reminder of the necessary safety procedures and put on my fins, before signalling to our colleagues that we were ready. We flipped backwards off the boat and began our descent into the lake. I was cheered by the fact that the sun had come out and the water was now a beautiful clear iridescent blue. This was a wonderful silent world. The only sound I was aware of was that of my own breathing and I watched my expired air bubbles rising to the surface, expanding and sparkling like crystal baubles. I was totally enthralled by this magical new world and quickly grew accustomed to the technique of pumping air into my suit to gain the buoyancy necessary as we reached new depths. Swimming felt effortless as movement of the giant fins propelled us along and downwards. After a matter of minutes, we reached a shelf at about twenty feet and I realised that this had been a path or roadway for access to the quarry. We then descended further into the pit and at about forty feet, we reached some old railway tracks. They were now very rusty and twisted, but it was obvious that on these, had run the trucks or bogeys which carried the hewn clay from the pit. Some of the old trucks remained as evidence of this former life. In the distance was an old, rusty, corrugated iron shack and we swam towards it. My buddy signalled several times to ask me if I was OK and I signalled that I was. It was a wonderful experience, but at this depth I was finding it hard work to keep going. Regardless of the quantity of air, which I pumped into my suit, I kept sinking into the white silt at the bottom. I had to fin hard to keep moving but found that if a fin touched the silt, it became stirred up giving me nil visibility. Several times I emerged from a cloud of silt and was relieved to see my buddy just ahead. We eventually reached the hut and he signalled to me to take it slowly as we approached the doorway. We used our underwater torches as we entered the gloom and suddenly a huge pike emerged from a dark corner, darted past us and swam off into the distance. I had never seen a pike at close quarters and couldn't help noticing rows of sharp teeth. I found myself giving a silent scream and my teeth clenched around my demand valve. My buddy had clearly known what to expect and seemed quite amused by my reaction. We explored the hut and surrounding area and then, after checking our air gauges, he signalled that it was time to surface. We slowly ascended by initially pumping air into our suits and then venting it as we neared the surface. I felt a little anxious as I remembered all the instructions to

182

breathe out as air expanded so as not to burst a lung and constantly equalise pressure in the ears so as not to burst an ear drum. It all made sense, but without having had the benefit of a training course, there seemed a lot for me to remember on this first dive. As we surfaced, I noticed that it seemed to be an effortless procedure for my buddy, while I was having to fin exceptionally hard to ascend, but I just assumed that as a novice, there was something that I hadn't got quite right. At last we saw the boat above us and with a few leg movements, my fellow diver finned his way to the surface, rose out of the water and over the side of the boat. He then leaned over and signalled to me to follow. It took me several attempts however to come alongside the boat and I had great difficulty in rising high enough to get over the side. Eventually, I found myself being unceremoniously hauled into the boat rather like a beached whale. My hood was removed and I gave everyone a big grin as I again breathed fresh air. I felt exhausted but exhilarated. I suddenly realised that once again, my colleagues were howling with laughter as gallons of water were seeping out of the seals in my so-called dry suit. The neck seal was too big for me and had leaked, so that my dry suit had become a very wet suit. The water had filled every unoccupied space in my boots and suit and weighed me down. Even when I pumped air in to gain buoyancy, little was achieved, so I had had to work double time to propel myself along. Not knowing what to expect, I had happily thought that everything was fine and that I just needed to improve technique. No wonder that I was totally exhausted! I laughed along with my new friends who welcomed me as their unofficial team member. I was keen to repeat the experience and it was agreed that, whenever I could get time off from my JLO duties on a Monday, I would join them on a training session.

Members of my team in JLO were very supportive of my ambition, although they probably thought that I was mad. I worked overtime as often as possible in order to be able to save sufficient hours to take time off to dive at least once a month. I decided never again to wear an ill-fitting dry suit, so I bought myself a wet suit. I also realised that if I wanted to dive again, without compromising every safety regulation in the book, that I needed some proper training. I now accepted that I would never be officially selected as a police diver and attend a national training course, so I decided on another course of action. I joined Bedfordshire Sub-Aqua Club and trained regularly in order to gain the standard scuba diving qualification. My husband, who disliked swimming and water sports, seemed to accept that I had taken up a new hobby, including me enjoying the sport during family holidays abroad. He seemed to turn a blind eye to the fact that on Mondays I would often come home from 'work' with wet hair and a bag of diving kit.

Over the period of the next ten months, I enjoyed many a dive with the police team, sometimes returning to the Blue Lagoon, but more often in the rivers, canals and other waterways of Bedfordshire. Regardless of the sense of humour displayed by my colleagues on that first day out, I found them to be very hard working and serious about their role in the Force. Their work was extremely varied, ranging from helping to recover sunken vehicles, often stolen, recovering bodies from accidents, murders or suicides, and searching for a wide range of articles used in crime. I thoroughly enjoyed the experience gained working with them, albeit in an unofficial capacity.

On one occasion, we were on a training dive in the River Ouse at Felmersham, when my colleague pointed to a small tote bag in the silt on the riverbed. We pulled it free and hauled it to the surface, where on examination, we found it to contain jewellery. This was later matched to a burglary, where the thief had taken a haul, but only wanted the better quality items and discarded the rest in the river. I like to think that some of those less costly items perhaps, when returned, at least had sentimental value to the victim. In any case, to me it was the nearest that I will ever get to discovering hidden treasure!

Sometimes, we didn't find quite what we were looking for, but there were always items of interest. At Wyboston, where the river winds its way past the Wyboston Lakes Golf Course, we were searching for a dumped motor vehicle, but instead found about fifty golf balls, a bent club, and a very reasonable golf trolley. I could only assume that a player was having a particularly bad game, lost his temper, broke his club and then decided to dispose of his trolley. The river hides many a tale.

The River Ouse forms a particularly attractive picture, as it flows through the town centre and adjacent Embankment gardens. This is an area for family walks, boating, regattas and annual river festivals. Sadly, it is also an area where drunks, returning from town centre pubs, sometimes decide to demonstrate their prowess by swimming across the river. Over the years, several have not made it and their bodies have subsequently been recovered. On one occasion, I was diving with the team under one of the bridges along the Embankment and we found a body. It was not that of the young man who we were looking for (he subsequently turned up safe) but that of a lady who had committed suicide. The body was recovered and although a gruesome sight, having been in the water for over a week, I did not find the experience any more upsetting than any other sudden death that I had attended during my service. This experience made me think that, given the chance, I could have coped with all the challenges of being a police diver.

Not all occasions were quite as gruesome and there were often moments of mirth, as the river revealed some of its secrets. On one occasion, whilst diving in the area of the Embankment after the dredgers had been at work, we uncovered a fine collection of old glass bottles, mostly

Victorian. Apparently, there had been a brewery close to this site at one time and the bottles bore the title and brewery crest. I had seen bottles of this type in antique shops but never in this quantity. There were bottles of green, brown or clear glass, many with marbles in the neck, and in a range of different shapes and sizes. The dredger had stirred up the mud, so visibility was very poor, almost nil. In order to recover the bottles, we swam along the bottom of the river-bed, squelching the mud through our gloved hands until we found a solid shape. Several times I came across small 'squidgy' items instead, but hastily dropped whatever it was back into the mud. I was having difficulty carrying all the bottles I found, but by a stroke of luck I came across a supermarket wire basket on the river bed. I loaded my haul of bottles into the basket and looked every bit the 'happy shopper' when I surfaced with the goods.

Whenever a job posed a special danger or there was a risk of water pollution, I observed the team and assisted the support crew rather than diving. My colleagues always behaved in a very professional manner and never exposed me to any unnecessary risks. I was conscious of the fact that if the Chief Superintendent had known of my escapades, he probably would have been furious with both my colleagues and me. I tried to be sensible by acquiring proper training, taking time off rather than using duty time, and never compromising the work of the team. Nonetheless, he was a strict boss and would not have taken kindly to my actions. I didn't want to get my colleagues into trouble, but there was one occasion where it was a bit of a close call. On a training day, I was diving with a buddy in the Blue Lagoon and we were coming to the end of our dive when the Chief Superintendent came to the site for an ad-hoc inspection visit. On observing his approach, the support team acted rapidly and a colleague brought an extra air cylinder and weight belt down to me and signalled that a senior officer was on site. I got the message, swapped cylinders and then swam onto a ledge, where I waited until the Chief Superintendent left the site

After a year, and many challenging but enjoyable diving experiences with the police diving team, I changed my role within the service. My new job did not allow me the flexibility to take time off on Mondays, so I was no longer able to join the diving team. Nonetheless, I retained diving as a hobby for many years to come and was satisfied that I had achieved my goal, albeit by backdoor methods. My secret concerning my diving escapades remained safe for the rest of my police service. I would be forever grateful to the colleagues who gave me the opportunity to dive with them and to those in the JLO team who covered for me during my absences. I never felt guilty about my diving activities, because within a few years, women were happily accepted as part of diving teams in Bedfordshire Police and other Forces. Diving never appeared on my Police Service record, but that did not matter to me. I had certainly reached new depths.

Chapter 13

Right Place, Wrong Time

There were times in my police career when I felt that I was an actress with a 'bit part' and had walked onto the stage at the wrong time.

From March 1984 until March 1985, the National Union of Mineworkers were engaged in a battle with Margaret Thatcher's Tory government and the full force of the state. It started when it was announced that Cortonwood Colliery in Yorkshire was to close and that twenty other pits and twenty thousand jobs were on a hit list. The Yorkshire miners' response was immediate and within six days the strike had spread nationally. Durham and Kent miners joined the strike, but Nottinghamshire miners were more reluctant. On 12 March, flying pickets arrived at the Nottinghamshire coalfield. Police from all forces were then required to provide mutual aid to deal with public order incidents arising from secondary picketing and the use of flying pickets.

Bedfordshire Police was no exception and provided mutual aid by sending Police Support Units (PSUs) to Humberside, Kent, Leicestershire, Nottinghamshire, South Yorkshire, Staffordshire and Warwickshire. On average, one hundred and fifty male officers were deployed on PSUs each week. The majority had received basic public order training, but were more used to community policing. They wore their normal uniforms, but had riot shields available.

I was working as a trainer at the time and felt left out when all the male Sergeants and constables from the department took their turn on the front line at the Miners' Strike. Women had been barred from PSU training, so were not to be utilised on mutual aid. I was required to stay behind to deliver Probationer Training or assist on division, where manpower was depleted. At the end of my normal duties, however, I was often required to act in a welfare capacity. Usually, accompanied by a traffic officer as driver, I went up to the police barracks, where officers were billeted to take supplies or to bring back officers who were sick, required at court, or when there was a crisis at home.

On one occasion, I drove up to a holiday camp at Cleethorpes in Lincolnshire, where our officers were billeted in the chalets. It was March and still very cold. When I arrived, I went to meet one of my colleagues who showed me their accommodation. The chalets were musty and damp, with very basic bathroom facilities. There were three or four police officers to a chalet and the more they tried to heat their chalets, the more the condensation increased and clothes were going mouldy. These were emergency conditions but I know I would have hated it.

When I asked to use the toilet, my fellow Sergeant said that it would be better for me to use the facilities in the main building. He made a quick phone call and then we strolled across to the large complex. He showed me through several doors and along a dimly lit corridor. He then pointed to another door and said "the ladies' is through there." I opened the door and walked through, but there was a bright light and it took my eyes a few minutes to adjust. I then realised with horror that I was standing on a stage in what had been the variety theatre and there was an audience of off duty policemen all sitting there in eager anticipation of entertainment. A sudden roar of catcalls and shouts of

"Get them off!" pounded in my ears and I just fled off the stage to laughter and cheers. Perhaps if I could sing or dance I might have done a turn, but instead the audience just got to watch a film as previously planned.

My colleague was nearly peeing himself with laughter, as he then showed me to the ladies room!

On one of my other visits, PSUs were staying at an Army camp, where they were accommodated on camp beds in the gymnasium. I arrived at the gatehouse after a long journey. I was in civilian clothes, so showed the sentry my police warrant card and rather jokingly said "I come to bring welfare to the men of Bedfordshire". He looked horrified, looked me up and down with a steely stare and said, "Not on my bloody watch you don't, lady".

I explained the actual purpose of my visit and was given entry to the camp. I was met by a Bedfordshire Inspector and went to see the accommodation. Men were already sleeping on long lines of camp beds with very little personal space and the odour of perspiration, flatulence and sweaty socks was overpowering. One man snoring is as much as I can take, but forty all at once was just too much! There were only two toilets in the block and they were both disgusting. Although I had felt as though I was missing out by not being allowed on the front line, I now decided that I was very fortunate not to be deployed alongside my male colleagues.

At that time, most police forces did not deploy women on the front line, but some of the city forces had women in their mounted sections and these were successfully deployed. I would witness many more changes in the role of police women, before my career ended.

I certainly never got bored during my police service as there were always new and varied challenges. Occasionally, there were special incidents or exercises organised by

Headquarters, involving all ranks, including our chief officers.

On one occasion, we all became aware that a major exercise was about to take place at an old aerodrome at Thurleigh in North Bedfordshire. Information was on a need to know basis and those officers detailed to be involved, attended a briefing. As a Sergeant, I was disappointed when my Inspector said I wouldn't be required for the exercise, so was to cover routine divisional patrol duties.

Thurleigh Aerodrome was a former RAF Bomber Command Station located five miles north of Bedford, near to the village of Thurleigh. In 1942 the aerodrome had been used by the USAF for heavy bomber operations against Nazi Germany. Since the end of WWII, Thurleigh became a research site for the Royal Aircraft Establishment (RAE). It had a ten thousand feet operational runway used for experimental development work. The site had its own security, but I had been there on a few occasions to liaise with security officers or to deal with break-ins at the adjoining small business park.

I knew that a request had gone out for constables willing to act as hostages during the exercise. There was plenty of speculation going on in the canteen, but I assumed that the exercise at Thurleigh aerodrome would be a terrorist situation with hostages on an aeroplane.

The exercise planning and logistics involved the Cabinet Office Briefing Rooms (COBR) at Whitehall. COBR gets involved in times of national crisis or emergency to coordinate actions of UK government bodies, so we knew something big was about to occur.

On the day of the exercise, I was Patrol Sergeant at Bedford. We were managing with a depleted section as we were sending lots of resources and manpower to Thurleigh.

I went out on patrol, but was called back to the police station to see the duty Inspector who instructed me to drive out to Thurleigh, deliver four extra radios required for use by the police teams and then return to Greyfriars as soon as possible.

On arrival at the aerodrome, I could see a plane on the runway and police and army vehicles around the perimeter. I parked my vehicle and then looked around, but couldn't find any police officers in the near vicinity, so I went straight to the control tower to deliver the radios. I went upstairs and entered the control room looking for a senior police officer. Instead, I found a team of Home Office officials and senior military officers, but no police officer. They didn't seem to notice my presence as they were all listening intently to a radio microphone, as an Arabic sounding voice shouting demands. I heard him say, "I want to speak to the senior police officer now!"

All eyes were suddenly on me, so I explained that I had only come to deliver some radios and was not involved in the exercise. A senior military officer said "Sergeant, as the only police officer present you had better speak to him, or he is going to start shooting the hostages". I didn't feel that I had any choice. I picked up the microphone and spoke to the terrorist. At his insistence, I gave my name, rank and number and not surprisingly he seemed offended by my low rank and the fact that I was a woman. He demanded that I go out to the plane within fifteen minutes or he would start shooting hostages. I had no idea of protocols, but knew that I should not be getting involved. I looked to others in the room for advice, but they all said that the decision was mine and then made copious notes. The Army officer offered me a military vehicle to take me out to the runway. In the circumstances, I decided that I had better go. A driver in a military vehicle took me to within a hundred yards of the plane and I then began to walk towards it. I became aware of some movement in the long grass and realised that there were firearms officers lying under cover.

As I neared the plane, I could see two men wearing balaclavas in the cockpit and terrified looking hostages looking out of the passenger windows. They had volunteered for the job, but it seems that the situation was becoming all too real for them. As I got closer, I saw a terrorist aiming a Kalashnikov AK47 rifle at me. He shouted, "Woman take off your hat and shoes". I complied and then kept walking. He shouted, "Now take off your jacket and tie". Again I complied, but started to wonder what was next and hoped that I was wearing attractive underwear. I presumed that the terrorist was just checking that I wasn't wearing a radio wire. I kept walking and arrived at the plane. I was then beckoned up the stairs by an agitated terrorist who jabbed me with a rifle and yelled demands. Even though I knew that this was an exercise, it felt very real and I was nervous in this very hostile situation. I didn't know what was going to happen to me, but I stayed calm as I knew that I had a job to do. I made mental notes of the number and descriptions of the terrorists and their weapons and tried to assess the hostage situation. Much to my surprise and great relief, I was given a list of demands and then allowed to leave and walk back to the control tower, picking up my clothes on the way.

On arrival at the control tower, a police senior officer was now in situ. He looked at me and said, "Where the hell do you think you've been?" I explained what had happened, but he was furious, telling me that I had gone against laid down protocols.

I felt like telling him that it wouldn't have happened if he had got there earlier, but I bit my tongue and kept my thoughts to myself. I was whisked away to another building by Special Branch, who carried out a full debrief. I was able to give them lots of useful information about the terrorists and the situation at the plane, but nobody said 'well done' or asked me how I was feeling.

I returned to Greyfriars Police Station and went to see the duty Inspector, He said, "Where the hell have you been. I told you to be quick!" I told him that I had been 'held up', but couldn't be bothered to tell him the whole story and went out on patrol.

There was eventually an exercise debrief, but I wasn't invited to attend. My part in the exercise was clearly an embarrassment to senior officers, so the less said the better. The exercise had been an opportunity for emergency services and armed forces to work together and test their resilience for a terrorist attack. In this scenario the Home Secretary had signed over responsibility from the police to the army. The police cordoned and contained the situation, enabling the army to bring the incident to a conclusion. The SAS stormed the plane, killed the terrorists and released the hostages.

Upon reflection, I realised that I had been in the right place at the wrong time, but nonetheless had found the scenario quite exciting. This was yet another true story to save and one day tell my grandchildren.

Chapter 14

Police Trainer

I was still keen to progress my career and have new challenges, so I applied to become a police instructor. I was selected and attended a ten-week intensive teacher training course at the National Police Training College at Pannal Ash, Harrogate. I found it quite emotional being away from my daughter during the week, but I knew that she was well cared for and I would see her most weekends. If I passed the course, it would be well worth the effort because most of my duties would be mainly 9 am – 5 pm for the next few years, I would spend more time with my daughter and do a job that I loved.

I didn't have a car and was the only Bedfordshire officer to be attending the course, so I travelled to Harrogate by train. Joining instructions had advised that each student instructor should bring uniform and, rather bizarrely, a typewriter. Apparently, there weren't enough at the centre, so each police force had to equip their own student. I was issued with a heavy old Imperial typewriter, which I then had to drag around with me on the train from Bedford to Harrogate. Together with my other luggage, this was a real stamina test, so I treated myself to a taxi from the railway station to the college.

There were five men and five women on our course, which was apparently a milestone for the training centre, as in the past, courses had been predominately male dominated. This was the first training course that I had ever been on where I felt that we were all treated as adults and equals. The course was intensive and we worked very long hours. Throughout the day, we learned how to present lessons on law and procedure. Then our evenings were spent preparing lessons for next day. That in itself wasn't a problem, but we also had to type our lesson plans, one for our own use and a carbon copy for class instructor. Like most of my colleagues, I wasn't a typist so the clackety-clack of two fingered typing went on late into the night. We were also expected to practice our delivery in front of a colleague, or the bathroom mirror. The walls of our bedrooms were very thin, so it was like living in a mad house!

I thought that being a mother was tiring, but this was nothing short of exhausting!

In addition to being assessed on our lessons, we were also marked on our appearance, so there was also lots of pressing uniforms and bulling of shoes.

We all worked as a team, supporting each other through difficulties, sometimes laughing at errors or applauding each other's successes. We had all come through an education system using blackboards and more recently flip charts, but new innovations were being introduced. In addition to developing our basic teaching skills, we had great fun with new technology and electronic white boards, which would wow our students, if our Forces could afford to buy them. Many of the new boards were also magnetic, so we put our art skills to good use by designing visual aids that could literally be thrown onto the boards. Teaching would never be the same again and in any case, within a short time, computers and PowerPoint would take over as the prime method of training delivery.

We all passed the course, becoming qualified police instructors. Most of us returned to our respective Forces to utilise our skills, but a few became instructors at regional training centres. That would mean long periods away from home, so I was glad to be returning to my Force. Applying for this course was one of the best decisions in my police service, as it gave me new skills and confidence that would open a number of doors in my life.

On completion of the course, I was posted as an Instructor in the Force Training Department, located at Bedfordshire Police Headquarters in Kempston. As a result of new legislation, changes in procedure or a need for personal development, all Bedfordshire police officers and civilian staff members attended training courses at HQ during their service.

Initially, I was the only female trainer and involved in delivering training on law and procedure to probationer constables. My posting to Training however coincided with a number of major changes in the police service, which were to have an impact on my role,

Following the Brixton Riots, the Scarman Report 1981, led to a recommendation for Community and Race Relations Training. I was required to plan and deliver the subsequent in-Force training programme. A basic structure was recommended by the Home Office and National Police Training and was to be delivered to all Bedfordshire Police officers and staff. This was a massive logistical exercise as abstractions for training could lead to policing shortages on division. It was also not a popular course to attend, as many officers took exception to the fact that the police generally had been branded as racists.

I knew that it was going to be a challenging subject to put over and that although I certainly did not consider myself as an expert on the subject, I would need to be convincing as a trainer. I submitted a request to attend a Race Relations course at the Police Staff College,

Bramshill in Hampshire. Bramshill was a fine Jacobean mansion owned by the Home Office and used as a college for higher police training. This included the six-month Junior Command Course for newly promoted senior officers and the Senior Command Course for those who were expected to achieve Chief Constable rank. There was also a Special Course for Sergeants, who were graduates and had been selected for accelerated promotion. In the 1980s, very few women attended Bramshill.

As British policing was considered by many to be the best in the world, Bramshill also ran Overseas Command courses, bringing senior officers from many countries.

Carousel Courses were relatively short and designed to meet the needs of a changing organisation, keeping senior officers up to date with changing law and procedure. I applied for a two week Race Relations Carousel Course and was accepted, so felt privileged to have the opportunity.

When I arrived at Bramshill and entered the gates leading to an impressive driveway, I felt as though I was entering a different world. There was a beautiful lake, woodland walks, a cricket club and white deer roaming the grounds. My first view of the Jacobean mansion filled me with awe.

I went to the reception area in the main building to book in. On giving my name, I was handed a room key, but then the receptionist said, "Oh Sergeant Groom, you are a woman. We will have to find you different accommodation, as you can't share a bathroom and showers with the men!"

I was soon given the front door key to a house located in the grounds. The house was reserved for women officers and visitors, but I had it all to myself for most of my course. Although, I would enjoy the opportunity to relax, I knew that there were times when I would miss the companionship of my male colleagues.

I took delight in exploring the fine Jacobean mansion, with its grand entrance hall and state rooms decked in fine tapestries, an oak panelled bar, resembling a traditional gentlemen's club and a long gallery which housed the National Police library.

On joining my course, I found that all my fellow students were male and either Chief Inspectors or Superintendents, so as a female Sergeant I was definitely the odd one out. Fortunately, both the students and the Syndicate Director were very friendly and treated me as an equal member of the group. In fact, when we were discussing equal opportunities, racial prejudice and discrimination, I had some interesting experiences and views to put forward. I've never been an overt feminist, but firmly believe in equal opportunities and promotion on merit. I learned a great deal from the course and realised that, although this would not have been my chosen specialist subject, I was well equipped and had the confidence to deliver the subject.

Whilst at Bramshill, there was a Formal Dining-in-Night and my course was invited. Evening dress was required so all the gentlemen on my course were suitably attired and I wore a red strappy evening gown. I was most impressed when I was told that the men would meet me at the door of my accommodation and escort me to dinner, which was held in the rather grand dining room. This was my first experience of formal dining and all its traditions. After the meal, I was bemused by the tradition of passing the port to the left and gentlemen only, so as it passed me by, I pointed out that I would like my glass filled. I enjoyed my port but suffered a rather haughty stare and some snide comments from one of the academic staff. When we all had a drink in hand, we stood for the Loyal Toast. It was then announced that there would be a comfort break before the speeches.

After dinner most of us retired to the bar, where we tended to sit in syndicate groups. There were probably about fifty men in the bar, including an Overseas Command Course. I was the only woman, but felt very comfortable sitting with my colleagues. There was a light-hearted atmosphere and lots of good natured joking. One of the men in another group called over saying, "You are lucky to have a woman in your group. Can we buy her off you for fifty camels?" I was not offended and laughed along with everyone else. I was surprised, however, when one of the men from the Overseas Command Course came over to our group and asked to be 'introduced to the lady'. I stood up, shook hands and chatted to him for a while and found out that he was a Swedish senior policeman called Bernard. I told him that it was a pleasure to meet him and then rejoined my group. At around 11 pm, I decided to leave the men to it, so said 'Good night' and stood up to leave. Bernard then came over and said "May I escort the lady to her accommodation". My male colleagues were highly amused and made some crude gestures, but I whispered, "Don't be so rude. I'm sure that he's just being the perfect gentleman. If he wants to escort me then that's ok". We left the main building and strolled through the gardens back to my accommodation, chatting about Bramshill, the weather and things in general. When I got to the front door of the house, I held out my hand to shake hands and said, "Good night and thank you". He shook my hand and held on to it and looked into my eyes and said, "Would you like a F...?" I wasn't sure that I heard right and said "Pardon?" He repeated himself and rather than slap him, I replied, "No thanks. I prefer to be in love with someone before I have sex!" He replied "Oh, in Sweden we f... for f...s sake!" I laughed and went in and locked the door, leaving him cooling off outside. I wanted to improve my education at Bramshill, but Swedish was not on the curriculum!

Later in my career, I returned to Bramshill for several short courses and found that the number of women students had increased. The new en-suite accommodation meant that male and female students could be housed together, both studying and socialising on equal terms.

Bramshill Staff College cost the Home Office about £5 million a year to run, so it was decided that it was no longer economically viable and in 2015 it was sold for around £20 million, ghosts and all!

On my return to the Force, I duly delivered the Race Relations Training to officers of every rank and civilian staff. I invited members of our local ethnic minority groups to participate in some sessions and put forward their experiences and views. There were some heated debates in the classroom, because in a police service that was still dominated by white males, many simply did not see a problem with the way we policed and felt that political correctness had taken over. I was of the opinion that most police officers were simply representative of the society that we live in, but they had to understand that although society might be racist, we had a professional requirement to be seen to be acting impartially. I also believed that regardless of their inherent prejudices, most police officers did not set out to discriminate against black people per se, but took action against people they believed to be criminals. They used experience and common sense to decide when and where to stop, check or arrest someone and this may unwittingly be disproportionate. The rules of engagement had changed, however, and police officers needed to act strictly within the new law, be aware of implications and be prepared to justify their actions.

In 1984 as a consequence of the Scarman Report and recommendations by the Royal Commission on Criminal Procedure, the Police & Criminal Evidence Act (PACE) was implemented. The purpose of the act and code of practise was to carefully balance the rights of the individual against the powers of the police. These include the much debated Stop and Search powers, Powers of Arrest & Detention and the Taping of Interviews. As trainers we were required to learn, interpret and teach the new law to every member of Bedfordshire Police, many of whom were against the changes. It was tiring and exacting work, because we had to try to win hearts and minds, or at least convince officers that they must adapt to these legal changes or risk losing their jobs.

I enjoyed the challenging work in the Training Department and certainly lost any fear I might have had about addressing senior officers and other groups on difficult subjects.

With my new-found confidence, I was ready to move on in my career. I had proved that I could combine my professional life with my role as a mother and now I just had to convince a promotion board.

Chapter 15

Pips, Pubs and Local People

I was a Sergeant for fourteen years, but attended another promotion board in 1987. My daughter was now six years old, so I figured that I had proved my ability to combine motherhood and a career. Every officer in the Force had a personal record which was stored in the Human Resources Department. I had viewed a copy of my record, which clearly stated that I had not been promoted because I had taken maternity leave. I now hoped that my career could move on.

With renewed enthusiasm, I attended a promotion board chaired by our new Deputy Chief Constable (DCC), who had recently served in Metropolitan Police and seemed to be very up to date on Equal Opportunities legislation.

Part of the way through the interview, I was being questioned; when the DCC glanced at my record and then asked me to confirm that in 1974 I had passed the Promotion Exam to Inspector and a promotion board in 1981. I agreed that this was correct and he then spoke to the other board members saying "Gentlemen, no further questions". He then thanked me for my time and I left the room, not quite sure what had happened.

Very soon afterwards, in October 1987, I received a letter from my Chief Constable, confirming my acceptance for promotion and almost immediately, I was promoted to Inspector and posted to Biggleswade Police Station. My family no longer lived there, but I still felt that I had a special affinity with this Bedfordshire market town.

My new warrant card now announced me as Inspector 1134 Groom. The change to my uniform on promotion was minimal – a silver braided bar under the hat badge and two Bath Stars or 'Pips' instead of Stripes.

Rather bizarrely all inspectors were also issued with brown leather gloves instead of black. This was clearly a military throwback, but considering that we wore black shoes and women were still issued with black handbags, it seemed a real anomaly. Visual changes may have been small, but there was a big leap in my self-esteem. I was now addressed as Inspector or Maam by officers of lower rank and I felt quite comfortable with this. I had waited a long time for promotion and was delighted to have the chance to prove myself.

Achieving the rank of Inspector was also like gaining entry to a private club, as I was now entitled to attend formal functions organised on behalf of the Senior Officers' Dining Club. The formal dinners were always black tie events and similar to the Armed Forces' Mess dinners. They were attended by the Chief Constable and most of his senior officers from Inspector upwards, as well a VIP guests such as the High Sherriff, Judges and local members of the aristocracy. I duly bought myself a wardrobe of evening gowns and began networking. I had to make up for all the missed opportunities to get to know senior ranks and their wives or partners in a social setting. The formal dinners were usually held at Police HQ, but on one special occasion, we dined in the Sculpture Gallery at Woburn Abbey, which was rather superb. Senior Officers each paid an annual membership to the dining club and then the cost of the occasion. It was all a new experience for me and I enjoyed the events, but there were many officers of various ranks who felt that such gatherings were elitist and outdated. I didn't agree, but egalitarianism eventually won the day and several years later the Senior Officers Dining Club was disbanded.

In February 1988, I attended a three-week Inspectors' Course at Hertfordshire Police Headquarters, Welwyn Garden City. The course not only taught the skills required of an officer, but ensured that we were mentally prepared for the challenges of leadership at this level. I was always fascinated by the personality tests that we took, while on this course. In the 'Briggs Myers Test' I came out as extravert, intuitive and judgemental. In the Belbin Team Role Test I was revealed as a creative person, who enjoyed implementing ideas, being in control and shaping outcomes, but could be impatient with others. I had to accept that this was a fairly accurate assessment. I am a real team player and good at utilising the skills of others, but I do like to be in charge and expect to get results. I hadn't really thought about my personality before taking these tests, but I was fairly comfortable with the person that I had become.

As an experienced trainer, I was confident in my ability to make decisions and deliver a briefing, but I knew that as a Sergeant I had very much enjoyed 'being one of the lads' and now I had to be more detached in my approach. Once again, I would learn to roleplay and project an appropriate image.

It was while I was on the Inspectors' Course that I first met Chief Inspector Martin Phillips, who had just become Hertfordshire Force Training Officer. Little did I know it then, but he would have an impact on my life in so many ways. I subsequently returned to Hertfordshire Police HQ as a course director on several Inspectors' Courses, each of three weeks duration. Martin and I became friends and when later my marriage was in difficulties, we became a cross-border liaison unit before the government had even heard of the term!

On my first day as Inspector at Biggleswade, I arrived at the Police Station and drove my car under the archway into the front yard, where the Chief Inspector and I both had allocated parking bays. Although, I knew the police station well, having started here as a Special Constable in 1968, I now looked at it through new eyes. The station was built in 1939 to replace the old police station opposite and was of attractive red brick, now adorned with two lovely hanging baskets. I noticed that the brass door handles had been polished and the entrance lobby was clean and tidy. There was a wooden bench for visitors and a traditional style counter behind which sat a police officer or civilian enquiry clerk and a telephonist. My office was on the opposite side of the yard above the arches, so I went there first to drop off my coat and brief case. I was already aware that the Chief Inspector was on annual leave, so I intended to get settled in and then go over to the main building to introduce myself. I knew that the minute my car had arrived, word would have gone out around the station to alert everyone. I'd been part of this early warning system in the past!

I had only just hung up my coat, when there was a knock on the door and one of the cleaning ladies came in carrying a small tray with tea in a china cup and saucer and biscuits on a plate. I knew that before long I would choose to be down in the kitchen making my own tea, where I could chat to everyone, but this was certainly a nice greeting. I chatted to her and said how pleased I was with my initial impression of the station, which looked well cared for. The praise left her positively glowing as she returned to her immaculate kitchen, where I knew the copper pipes were always gleaming. On a small station like

Biggleswade, the civilian support staff tended to be local people, who took a real pride in their work and were important members of the team. This was particularly the case with the two female civilian Enquiry Office Assistants, who worked opposite shifts and would often be the only person on station when the officers were all out at jobs. They answered the telephones, dealt with enquiries at the front desk and acted as radio operators, so they were the interface between the police and the public. They also both had excellent local knowledge, which was a real asset. Together with the part time telephonist, the caretaker and the cleaners, I knew that these were important employees and could also be good allies for me in my new role.

I spent my morning looking around the station, introducing myself and discussing operational issues with the duty Sergeant. The station still had its original cells in use, with their green and cream tiled walls, wooden benches and heavy metal flaps on the doors. They were unoccupied at that time and in any case, Biggleswade only held prisoners for a short time, before transferring them to Greyfriars Police Station, court or prison.

I saw the morning shift as they paraded off duty and the afternoon shift as they paraded on and received a briefing. I told them that my door was always open and that they could come and see me if they had any problems or issues they wished to discuss. Ten minutes later, I was in my office, when a PC came up and asked to discuss a problem. I was pleased with myself to think that he was going to confide in me so soon. Then, he told me that the problem was the men's toilets, which were filthy and disgusted the men who had to use them. It wasn't quite the high profile operational issue that I'd like to cut my teeth on, but I would certainly be judged on how I dealt with it. I went straight over and checked the toilets, which were encrusted in years of grime and smelled terrible. There was a male cleaner responsible for these and the outside drains and he clearly was not doing his job. Word had it that he was lazy and usually spent his time reading men's magazines. I called him into the toilets and ordered him to get scrubbing. I warned him that I would be back in two hours to inspect his work. After one hour I was called over to the main building as all the staff were in tears. These were not tears of joy, but watering eyes due to fumes from the copious quantity of bleach that had literally been thrown up the walls in the men's toilets! Manual work didn't come easy to our male cleaner and it took me several formal warnings and the required paperwork to get rid of him. The lady cleaners applied their usual high standards, the men's toilets were eventually spotlessly clean and I think I passed my first test as an Inspector.

Biggleswade appeared to be a 'thirsty town', as it and the surrounding area had one hundred and seventeen public houses and as the local Inspector, my duties included that of Licensing Officer. In comparison to Bedford, Biggleswade was a relatively quiet town. We didn't have late nightclubs and most people made their way peacefully home after an evening at the pub. The town centre was usually deserted by midnight.

Routine visits to public houses were usually made by my Sergeants to check for underage or after hours drinking, but as Licensing Officer, I also visited many of the pubs before a licence came up for renewal or if there were specific problems. I was generally treated with respect by licensees and most of their customers, but sometimes being a female in uniform meant that I was mistaken for a 'kissogram' It's surprising how three pints can aid the imagination of some men!

I soon learned to brazen it out or to use humour and have a few quick responses, which would get their mates laughing, such as "You couldn't afford me darling" or "Be careful or you'll spend a night at my place – in a cell!" Laughter was often my friend in these situations, but occasionally, it was with a sigh of relief that I got out with my clothes on and without having to resort to strong-arm tactics!

As Licensing Inspector, I attended Biggleswade Magistrates Court at the Licensing Sessions known as Brewster Sessions and at other times when special licences were being applied for. My previous experience as Court prosecutor meant that I was confident in presenting facts and making objections before the court, but I had to study the Liquor Licensing Laws in much greater detail than I had ever anticipated. I got to know members of the Licensed Victuallers Association (LVA) and even enjoyed the annual LVA Ball, although I made sure that I paid for tickets and stayed relatively sober! Once again, there was a certain amount of roleplay necessary to maintain the necessary public image.

Dealing with accidents on the A1 was routine work for our patrol officers. In the case of a major pile up, specialist officers from the Road Traffic Department would either take over or assist at the scene. My job was to maintain an overview of all our commitments. Sometimes I went to a scene to check that we had enough resources and that diversions were in place and working effectively. Then, I would retire gracefully, appreciating that this was not my area of expertise and a senior officer at a scene can be a pain in arse!

The priority at that time was to keep traffic moving. Officers would mark and photograph the scene and keep at least one lane open, while recovery vehicles cleared the scene and the accident investigation took place. That is not necessarily the case today, where roads are closed for long periods while more sophisticated accident investigation techniques are used.

A lot of our work on the sub-division was very routine. The Chief Inspector and I would work opposite shifts and days off, so I had a good degree of autonomy both in organising our resources and dealing with the public.

I dealt with correspondence and complaints, issued personal cautions and was available to meet members of public coming into the police station. I am a firm believer in personal accountability and the need to be accessible, so feel very sad that, for financial reasons, so many police stations have closed their front offices in recent years.

I really relished my Inspector's community policing role and enjoyed participating in local events both on and off duty. On one occasion, I received a very late request from Biggleswade Carnival Committee in respect of the carnival parade that was taking place that same day. The organisers had just realised that, due to an administrative error, they did not have the essential police escort for the carnival parade. An urgent meeting took place and I agreed to cut out the usual bureaucracy and send a front and rear escort. With limited resources and only one hour to spare, I joined the station staff in cutting greenery in the station yard. We then fixed branches and balloons to the police escort vehicles and added notices reading 'Police Special Branch'. Our efforts caused much amusement during the parade and I think it was good public relations to show that we had a sense of humour.

Biggleswade area is predominately a rural market gardening area and there was a large agricultural college at Shuttleworth, Old Warden. An impressive annual country fayre was held there and local police provided officers to patrol the grounds and the perimeter as well as assisting with traffic control on the approach roads. When duty time permitted I would enjoy a visit to meet local craftsman, traders and farmers, but more often, it would be on my day off enjoying a great day out with the family.

On the adjoining site to the Agricultural College was Old Warden Aerodrome and the famous Shuttleworth Collection, one of the most prestigious aeronautical collections in the world, due to the variety of old and well-preserved aircraft. It was always a pleasure to meet the enthusiasts who took great pride in renovating aircraft to original standard.

There were on average, twelve air displays each year including evening displays. Police officers were required for traffic control duties, but this was an enjoyable duty as the officer also got to see the air display. Either the Chief Inspector or I were on duty to co-ordinate the police response in case of an accident or incident involving the public. There were occasional incidents, but fortunately not on my watch. If not at Old Warden, I could watch the air display from my office window as the planes flew over the town.

Incidentally, I did attend the crash of a microlight in a field nearby in which the pilot was killed. I dealt with the incident with Air Investigation Branch and realised just how fragile these machines could be. It was then a twist of fate, when in the same week I attended a Rotary Charity Ball and won a microlight flight in the auction. I did take the flight and thoroughly enjoyed it, but was slightly nervous when signing the insurance documents!

My story continues on a theme of transport and now relates to the River Great Ouse which flows through Bedfordshire, linking Bedford via a series of locks with the Wash on the Norfolk coast. It's a dream for many people to hire a narrow boat and take a relaxing journey along this scenic route. Two male pals decided to do just that and hired a boat from Priory Marina, Bedford. After receiving basic instructions, they were told to be careful of the low bridge at Great Barford, located half way between Bedford & St Neots. The early 15th century Barford Bridge is a Grade 1 listed Ancient Monument and spans the River

Ouse with seventeen arches. This scenic spot is made all the more attractive by the Anchor Inn, overlooking the bridge, so it gets very busy in the summer months.

When our two friends in their rented barge reached the bridge, one was steering and the other was standing on the side ledge. He stuck his head out to look at bridge and the last thing he was heard to say was "They warned us of the low bridge, but it's not that low!" The boat carried on, but unfortunately his head didn't as it struck a low arch.

It was a tragic accident, but like any sudden death it had to be investigated in order to establish the cause of death. I called out the Search and Recovery team and then went to the scene to oversee proceedings. It was necessary to close the waterway until police divers finished their grisly task of locating the deceased man's head. In police terms, closing a road or motorway was fairly routine, but closing a river or canal was a new one for me. The Great Ouse River Authority took appropriate action and we notified other police forces en route of the reason for closure. The subsequent enquiries and investigation were surreal. We had to protect the scene, interview witnesses and secure evidence. I set up a temporary incident room in the Anchor Inn, although refreshments for police officers were limited to coffee and sandwiches. It was a lovely summer's day so the pub garden became particularly busy with people enjoying the sunshine and a few pints of beer. People always seem to be fascinated by police action, but in this case we closed the footpaths and tactfully dissuaded interested onlookers. The Press and photographers soon arrived, so also had to be managed. A lot of police work involves learning by experience and this was no exception. The subsequent inquest found the cause of death to be accidental.

Biggleswade is an arable farming and market gardening area, so it attracted gypsies and travellers. Some came to work but pitched up on public or private land without authority. Removal is slow legal process and prosecution is rare, but generally speaking all local residents want is to see the temporary visitors move on. We did our best with limited resources and liaison with other agencies.

Police are usually far from welcome on the temporary sites, so even in police uniform, it felt intimidating surrounded by a hostile crowd and fierce dogs. Being able to stay calm but authoritative in such circumstances was a learned skill.

My sub-division included Potton, a small town of approximately five-thousand residents in the heart of rural Bedfordshire. It was the location of an official gypsy and travellers' site with around thirty caravan pitches, complete with concrete built toilets and laundry rooms.

The site gradually became unmanageable and major issues occurred, especially with vehicle crime and antisocial behaviour. The toilet blocks became scrap metal stores. Local residents became increasingly angry, although travellers claimed that complaints were unfounded or exaggerated.

Whatever the facts, this was an important local issue. I agreed to go along to a public meeting with the local beat officer to discuss issues and help to develop an action plan. There was a lot of anger, as people thought that their peaceful way of life was being eroded and the price of their home and property was being devalued.

The meeting became quite heated and I stood to address the audience, expecting to have a rough time. I outlined the issues and explained that statistics showed a relatively low level of crime in Potton. Presumably, this indicated a degree of under-reporting by residents who felt intimidated. I ended by saying "I don't come to you as a 'Knight in Shining Armour' to solve all your problems alone, but if you report incidents when they occur, I can and will work with you to deal with them".

A nervous resident stood and said loudly, "We are grateful to you for coming and listening to all our problems and we certainly regard you as our 'Shite in Nining Armour'! I smiled and replied that I resembled that remark and the audience collapsed in laughter. The angry mood was defused and the question and answer session continued in a much more positive tone. One again, I felt that humour had saved the day.

It was never easy visiting traveller sites, as police were quite clearly unwelcome guests and more often than not our visit included an investigation into an allegation of crime. At Biggleswade, however, I felt as though I had a 'go-between' who proved a real asset when a site visit was necessary or desirable. PC Loveridge was proud of his Romany-Traveller background and although some Travellers might have regarded him as a turncoat, he did have some useful contacts on the sites. One day, we drove through the Potton site in his patrol car and received some hostile looks and gestures, but on arrival at a Romany caravan, we were invited inside. The caravan was ornate and immaculate and the old lady made us tea, while we talked. I felt privileged to be her guest and realised that wherever you go in life, contacts are very important. When we left the caravan and walked through the site, it did seem that we were then treated with less suspicion and hostility.

PC Loveridge worked at one of our sub-stations located in a police house. One Christmas, after his shift finished, he invited me and a group of his colleagues to the police station for a Christmas lunch, which he cooked in the kitchen. It was a fabulous meal, including pheasant, duck, rabbit and other game. He told us that he had left hedgehog off the menu, although he did have an excellent recipe!

My role as Station Inspector gave me the opportunity to meet representatives of many different sectors of the local community and I always felt very honoured to represent

Bedfordshire Police at public events. I always wore my uniform with pride and was very much aware that even if I was nervous, the public had high expectations of a police officer in uniform and I must try and meet those expectations. I felt very humble when I was invited to lay a wreath at the town war memorial on Remembrance Day, as I knew that I was representing all those officers who had served their country.

By the middle of 1989, I was going through a divorce and submitted a report to my Chief Constable, stating that I intended to marry Martin Phillips, who was now a Superintendent in Hertfordshire Police. In those days marital difficulties and divorce were frowned upon and I knew that our news would not go down well at Bedfordshire or Hertfordshire Police headquarters. Martin was subsequently moved to the far end of his county, making it more difficult for us to spend time together. Nonetheless, we were married on 21st November 1989 and I became Mrs Phillips or Inspector 1311 Phillips. Martin and I bought our first home together in Biggleswade and my daughter Michelle, who was now eight, came to live with us and went to school in the town.

I was very happy living and working in Biggleswade, which gave me chance to spend more time with my family, further integrate in the community and make friends outside the police service. This was probably the most settled period in my career.

When our duties allowed, Martin and I enjoyed a good social life and attended a wide range of events in and around Bedfordshire. My role at Biggleswade meant that I was invited to become a member of the Friendship Club at nearby RAF Chicksands, which was then a base for USAF personnel. Martin and I were teamed up with three American families from the base and regularly met for social events at the base, local pubs or each other's houses.

I had visited Chicksands many times on duty and formally liaised with senior officers or USAF Police on a regular basis, but now I felt like a member of this big, very hospitable family. Although the base was in Bedfordshire, a social visit there was rather like visiting the United States, especially when watching a baseball game, attending the July 4th celebrations, or joining a family for Thanksgiving. Being invited to these occasions was a real treat for Martin, Michelle and me and I felt very fortunate to have a fulfilling job, which gave me such opportunities.

In 1990, after two years at Biggleswade Police Station, I was posted back to Greyfriars Police Station as a uniform patrol Inspector. Having had a high degree of autonomy as the only Inspector on Biggleswade sub-division, I now viewed this move as a retrograde step, but perhaps it was the penalty I had to pay for my new domestic bliss.

At Greyfriars, I was now one of team of four Inspectors, each covering one of the operational patrol sections on twenty-four-hour shift patterns. There was a hierarchy of Chief Inspectors, Superintendents and a Chief Superintendent, so I had to get used to taking the corporate line. I did particularly enjoy night shifts, when as Inspector, I was the most senior officer on duty. In any case I'm a bit of a 'night owl', so much to the dismay of my section, I was always wide awake. When I had been a young patrol officer on nights, I was aware that the duty Inspector would often be asleep in his office, with instructions that he was only to be woken if necessary. I was determined that I would never be like that, so when I came on duty I would get an overview of incidents in progress, attend the section briefing, check any urgent reports, deal with any prisoner reviews and then get out on patrol for a few hours.

I intended this to demonstrate my support of officers out on the streets, rather than checking up on them, but it did serve both purposes. At 3 am on a cold dark night, I was driving around a factory estate in an unmarked car, when I saw a panda car parked up in a corner. I could just see the silhouette of the driver who was slumped over in his seat. I parked up, walked over to the police car and then pulled the driver's door open. The officer tumbled out of the car and awoke with a start to see me standing over him with an angry look on my face. I said, "I will see you in my office in fifteen minutes!" and then drove off. I wasn't really angry, but needed to make the point that I expected my officers to be working not sleeping and had it been a criminal opening the car door, the outcome might have been different. The officer returned to the station and told his radio control colleagues what had happened. Needless to say, they laughed at his discomfit and my displeasure. I kept a straight face while I admonished him and off he went to warn the others about the dragon!

I had served at Greyfriars as a WPC, as a Sergeant and now as Inspector, so it did feel rather like my second home. I enjoyed being in charge of a section of three Sergeants and about fourteen officers. That sounds a lot, but three constables would be acting as radio operator, gaoler and enquiry officer. There would also usually be absences due to sickness, annual leave, court appearances or training commitments. Officers would also be engaged at the station dealing with a prisoner or writing reports, so we were lucky if we had six or eight officers out on the streets of Bedford, or patrolling the north of the county.

A summary of all incidents of note or arrests made during the shift were recorded in the Inspectors' Book, which could be used for reference by the incoming Inspector, especially if there were follow up enquiries or arrests to be made during the next shift. There were no linked computer records for the Force, so a night report would also be sent by telex to HQ for the attention of the Chief Constable.

In addition to running a patrol section, I gained useful experience from attending meetings with the Divisional

217

Command Team, where I began to learn more about policy and budgets. I was never afraid to ask questions or put forward suggestions and I found that I was treated with respect by my male colleagues. I began to realise that I felt comfortable working alongside senior officers and given the opportunity, I would enjoy further promotion.

It was a proud moment in 1991, when I received the Police Long Service and Good Conduct Medal, which at that time was awarded for twenty-two years of long and meritorious service. I sometimes thought that just meant that I hadn't been caught breaking any of the rules!

My father, my husband Martin and my daughter Michelle were at the medal ceremony with me. I was very much aware that without their ongoing support, I could not have enjoyed my career, achieved promotion and enjoyed family life.

In his citation my Chief Superintendent commented that I was the first Bedfordshire policewoman to take maternity leave and return to work, the first female station and Custody Sergeant and the first female trainer in Bedfordshire. He felt that I had taken a very active role in helping Bedfordshire Police move towards greater equality. I was flattered by his comments, but in my opinion there was still a challenge ahead. Bedfordshire Police did not have any female officers in their senior ranks.

Chapter 16

Full Circle

My career finally took some big steps forward and I broke through the glass ceiling, which at times for me had felt a bit more like concrete!

In 1992 I was given the opportunity to perform Acting Chief Inspector Duties, co-ordinating the work of the four sections at Greyfriars Police Station and becoming more involved in strategy meetings. Not perhaps the most exciting time in my career, but nonetheless, a useful experience. Alongside my police duties, I was informed that the role also included being Greyfriars police station bar manager. I held the master key and my job was to arrange the duty rota for the civilian bar staff, check that all deliveries were on schedule, ensure that a well stocked bar would be open for officers coming off duty or on rest days. Some might have regarded this as my most important job, as the bar was the hub of social life for most section officers. We celebrated birthdays, weddings, divorces, good arrests or convictions, but also provided support and informal counselling for anyone who had experienced a traumatic incident, been injured on duty or had simply had a bad day. Senior officers would often join the men and women at the bar and deliver thanks for a job well done.

A year later I was posted back to Headquarters Training Department as Inspector, co-ordinating the work of all the training staff. Having learned some new skills at Greyfriars, I now also took on the role of bar manager for our HQ bar and social club. This was a much larger concern, as the main canteen area at HQ was like the hub of the family and sometimes catered for dances, weddings, retirement parties and the Senior Officers Dining Club. I enjoyed many a Friday evening there, socialising with my husband, colleagues and their families. My daughter Michelle enjoyed playing with the other children and it was a chance for us all to relax.

The social life also extended to an annual Bedfordshire Police Sports Day on the field adjacent to HQ. There were traditional sporting events for members of the Force and their families, mini fairground rides for the children and displays by the dog section, diving team and firearms team. All serving officers paid a regular levy to the Sports and Social Club and this was the big free event of the year, much looked forward to by officers and civilian staff from all over the county. It was one of the rare occasions when off duty officers of all ranks met up and had fun together.

In 1996, I passed another Promotion Board and received a notification from my Chief Constable that I would be promoted to Chief Inspector as soon as a vacancy arose. Coincidentally my Chief Constable Mr Dyer was about to retire at that time. Although he had refused to promote me for many years, I still held him in high esteem. When I heard that I was about to be promoted by the incoming Chief Constable, I went to see My Dyer with a request that he promote me before he left. He understood the irony of this and said that it would be a pleasure to do so as his last formal duty. He told me that he had changed his views and thought that I had managed to successfully combine being a good mother and a good senior police officer. His comments meant a great deal to me because, although it had taken a long time for me to gain acceptance, I knew that the struggle had been worth it and the organisation had taken a big step forward. I felt sure that in future, maternity would not automatically be a bar to promotion.

Before he left, Mr Dyer promoted me to Chief Inspector and I remained in the post of Force Training Officer. I now planned the Force training strategy to meet the changing needs of the organisation. I introduced a management development programme and set up a resource centre for computer-based training. I realised that we couldn't keep taking officers away from their divisions for training new law and procedure and that some of it could be delivered and assessed as computer packages. I drew up building plans for an extension to the training wing, listed all the requirements and provided basic costs. The County Architect's Department formalised my plans, which I then submitted with a proposal to the Home Office and secured generous funding for the project. My workload was then doubled and I hit the ground running as I learned all about project management and oversaw the building and installation of the new resource centre. I came to realise that if you have a dream and the passion to carry it through, others will eventually be convinced.

In the first year of the new resource centre, we were visited by Her Majesty's Inspector of Constabulary, who commented favourably about the project in his annual report.

I prefer plain speaking and don't particularly like management speak, but as I was delivering lessons on management, there were times when I thought I had swallowed the complete dictionary of jargon! We would brainstorm ideas, look at a whole raft of opportunities, run ideas up the flagpole, do a cost benefit analysis, drill down and give ballpark figures before finally implementing robust plans!

The training staff comprised a team of eight police trainers, a physical training instructor (PTI), four civilian information technology trainers, a resource manager and an office manager. When new laws or procedures were introduced, it was our job to ensure that all relevant staff received the training, either on a course at HQ, on Division during shifts, or using computer technology. My experience gave me a good understanding of operational requirements, so I worked closely with divisional senior officers to maintain a balance between divisional needs and training needs.

This was also a time for introducing more rigorous physical fitness standards for operational officers. All of my trainers were keen to set a good example. The PTI suggested that we all went on a fitness regime and weight loss programme and we agreed. He recommended the cabbage soup diet, which seemed to be in vogue at the time. It involved making a huge pan of vegetable soup and consuming it at every meal. I joined the initiative and attended PT sessions in the gym. The 'Bleep test' had just been introduced, requiring officers to run to and fro along a fifteen-metre track in time with a series of bleeps. The timing between bleeps is slow at first but the bleep becomes faster as the test progresses and it becomes more difficult to keep up with the required speed. Basically, you run until you drop, but have to complete a minimum number of shuttles to pass. I don't mind admitting that I found it exhausting! Even worse, when we were doing press-ups and setups all those on the cabbage soup diet sounded like the trumpet section of an orchestra, which the men found hilarious. I decided that I had urgent work to do in the office!

Although I had always been fit enough to do my duty I had never been athletic or given much time to physical fitness regimes. Both on Division and at HQ, if I had any time in my refreshment break or after work I would enjoy a game of table tennis, but found that my busy work and home life didn't leave much time for sports other than swimming and occasional sub aqua diving. I realised that nearly all my male colleagues who were senior officers seemed to find time for badminton during a long lunch break and days off for representative sport playing cricket or golf. If I were giving advice to a young woman now, I'd recommend that they take up one of those sports, because I now realise that was where the male bonding took place and perhaps promotions were made or lost. I was once invited along to a two-day golf tournament by a senior officer, but when I explained that I didn't play golf, it soon became apparent that my golfing ability was not the issue. I politely declined!

Divisions had gymnasiums which were used for fitness, self-defence and public order training, but in my days these changing rooms were only equipped for men and the women had to change in the ladies toilets.

As a young Sergeant on division, I was going to play table tennis in a gym, which was accessed through the men's changing room. I knocked on the door, waited and then walked in just as three officers of senior rank emerged stark naked from the shower. I averted my glance (after a quick peek!) and carried on into the gym. A few hours later, I had a call from the Superintendent, asking me to go up to his office. I rather cheekily replied "I think I've already seen enough of you today Sir". Fortunately, he was amused!

My attitude to sport had been that it should be challenging but fun, whereas, I was now entering a world where the PTI shouted about running through the pain barrier. As he was now on my staff, I suggested that we could be kind to each other, especially since all good female runners were slim hipped and small breasted and I was neither! If I had half-an-hour free at lunch time and needed to clear my head, I used to go for a brisk walk around the sports field at HQ, only breaking into a jog when I felt that nobody was watching. I certainly never looked at my best all hot and sweaty in sports gear and preferred to maintain a professional image. On the other hand, I didn't mind watching the rippling muscles of some of our more athletic male officers!

As Head of Training, I managed a sizeable training budget and took an active part in the organisation's strategy meetings. All the management theory I had learned was now put into practice. If I didn't understand something at a meeting, or needed clarification, I would ask questions, or suggest that a cost-benefit analysis should be carried out. This sometimes infuriated the Chief Constable, who was trying to push through a project without argument. One of my senior colleagues suggested to me that I would need to keep my head below the parapet if I wanted to get on, which of course was like a red rag to a bull. Those comments made me smile, as it seemed I'd come a long way since my early days as a WPC at Training School, when an instructor told me that I'd have to learn to speak up for myself or I'd never get on. Thank goodness I could still laugh at myself.

One day the Chief Constable called me into his office and wanted my opinion on a project that he had in mind. He told me that he was asking me because he knew that I would give him an honest opinion. I took that as a real compliment and knew that I sometimes got away with being challenging because I was a woman. Sometimes, there are just too many Alpha males in an organisation!

The Chief Inspector's role also meant more training for me, as duties now included Public Order Incident Commander. Training involved learning to deal with public order situations, riots and petrol bombs. The public order protective gear was not exactly flattering. It was necessary to wear cotton undergarments and a cotton T-shirt, as manmade fibres can melt and stick to the skin. Kevlar body armour was worn under a flame-retardant overall and the outfit was completed by a flame-retardant balaclava, gloves, a riot helmet with communications and a pair of black boots with steel toe-caps. When in a public order situation, officers would also usually carry a short round or long rectangular shield as protection from missiles and firebombs. This was all a far cry from the skirt and stockings that I wore in the early days of my service, but it proved to be essential in public order situations. Not only did I find the body armour uncomfortable, but the whole outfit was totally impracticable for a woman who needed a pee! I also had an additional problem, as I had reached the menopause with its associated difficulties including occasional hot flushes. There was no way that I was going to discuss this with any of my male colleagues, as it would sound like female whingeing or making excuses. I decided to grin and bear the discomfort until I could see a doctor and get prescribed Hormone Replacement Therapy. As always, I felt that life was so much easier for a man.

I had gone through my police service without any Public Order Training, as women were barred from doing so, but now I was part of a new ball game. It wasn't easy to start such rigorous training at the age of forty-five, but I knew that it was essential if I wanted my career to progress. For normal police duties, I had started to wear police issue spectacles with varifocal lenses, but I found that they steamed up under a riot helmet. My public order role necessitated that I was capable of reading maps and other documents, so I changed to contact lenses, but found that after hours in a hot, dry situation, these dried up and caused discomfort, I think that it was only bloody-minded determination that kept me going.

Chief Inspectors trained with other ranks at the Metropolitan Police training ground at Hounslow, known as 'Riot City', as well as regular training in Force.

At Hounslow, training always began with a 'warm up' run in full kit around the streets of the mock city, with its roads, buildings and street furniture. Then, we took it in turns to act as rioters, throwing bricks at the line of riot police. Instructors would then throw petrol bombs at the line of officers. Our leather boots sometimes caught fire and we could feel the heat of the flames licking our overalls. The main thing was to stay together and stay calm, as each unit had officers equipped with fire extinguishers, so we could assist each other. It was a real lesson in team work and gave us confidence to deal with most situations.

During the training, Chief Inspectors also learned about strategy and tactics and would exercise and be assessed in deploying their units. Although I completed the required training, I was exhausted, but wasn't going to admit it! If ever there was a time in my service that I felt like the weak link, this was it. I hadn't anticipated this when I volunteered for equality in 1974 and probably wouldn't have chosen it now, but times and policing methods had moved on. Over the years, women would increasingly be deployed on the front line of policing and train alongside their male colleagues.

I knew that if I wanted further promotion, I not only had to be good at my job, but needed something a bit extra to get ahead of my male colleagues. I heard about a new Policing Degree being introduced at Portsmouth University and managed to get my Force to sponsor me. In addition to working long hours, I studied Psychology, Sociology and Criminology and eventually gained a BSc Honours Degree. Once that went on my CV I felt that I was ready for another promotion board, but I realised that there was hot competition, from both internal and external applicants.

It had come to my attention that some male officers who had been identified as having potential for senior ranks had received mentoring or support to prepare them for promotion. I had never received that kind of support in my career. I had always relied on self-motivation and been prepared to accept rejection. This time, I made up my mind to find myself a mentor. There were no women officers above the rank of Chief Inspector, so I decided to ask a male Superintendent to be my mentor. As an external candidate, he had passed the same Chief Inspectors' Promotion Board as me, joined Bedfordshire Police on promotion and gone on to achieve the next rank. In my opinion he was smart, confident, articulate and now stood out as someone who had all the skills and abilities to progress a long way in the organisation. He very kindly accepted the role of mentor and we met once a week to prepare me for the promotion board. He was both challenging and supportive and gave me some excellent advice. The promotion board would consist of practical exercises and scenarios, followed by an interview board comprised of male senior officers. My mentor taught me to think more like a man, being prepared to 'blow my own trumpet' and talk positively about my achievements and future plans. This did not come naturally, as I saw myself more as a team player, but I followed his advice when I appeared before the board. I think I sounded more commanding and more arrogant, but it seemed to impress the board as I passed the selection process. In January 1999, I finally achieved my goal and was promoted to Superintendent.

To my delight, I was posted back to Greyfriars Police Station in Bedford as Superintendent in charge of Operations for the Division. This was the station where I had started as a Special Constable, worked as a young policewoman and served at various ranks, so I felt very proud to be returning as Superintendent. I was also glad to be returning to operational policing.

The Superintendent's rank meant that others would treat me differently regardless of how I felt about the role. As well as increased responsibility, my new role came with the perks of a car allowance, a car parking bay in the police station garage, a secretary shared with the Divisional Commander and a large office with private bathroom. Perhaps some of these perks were becoming outdated in the modern police service, but I'd waited a long time to get to this rank and was going to enjoy it to the full!

The day I arrived at Greyfriars, I went up to my office and got quite a surprise when I opened the door. Instead of the usual cream and brown decor, my office was painted a soft shade of pink and there were flowers in a vase. Some might think that this was sexist, but I was delighted. I loved the kind thought and sense of humour and settled in very quickly to work with a great team of male and female officers.

As the Superintendent, I still enjoyed retaining a degree of femininity and a sense of humour, but sometimes it was necessary to roleplay the part. There's an expectation that a Superintendent will be serious, calm and decisive and that is what I became.

Fortunately, the Divisional Commander was a man who had his feet firmly on the ground. He had also worked his way up through the ranks and had known me for many years, so in private we were able to relax and share the occasional joke.

My Operational Commander's role included maintaining standards and discipline on division. It was often necessary to project a stern, professional image and occasionally put the fear of god into someone.

Officers who breached the discipline code would be called into the office and be required to stand to attention in front of the desk. I used to wear varifocal spectacles, which could be used to good effect because, if worn on the end of my nose, they made me look very serious. I still smile about an occasion when I dealt with a discipline matter involving one of our constables, who was charming, but who had a relaxed attitude to his paperwork. He had failed to submit some important reports, which could lead to loss of a conviction in court. I wanted to ensure that he understood the gravity of the situation, so I made him wait while I finished signing some papers and then gave him a very stern warning. I then dismissed him and told him to get out and get back to duty. As he left, he suddenly popped his head back round the door, waited for my attention and then said, "I just wanted you to know Ma'am that I've still got the hots for you!" For once I was lost for words and couldn't get angry, as I was both amused and flattered. Even policemen have their fantasies!

On another occasion when I reprimanded an officer for unprofessional conduct during a rather silly incident, he said "With all due respect Ma'am, I don't think you've got a sense of humour." I replied, "Probably not," but was delighted that all my past indiscretions had remained secret!

Also in 1999, I was fortunate enough to be nominated to attend the Women of the Year Luncheon at the Savoy Hotel, London. It was a fabulous day out and a great honour to be with so many women achievers from all walks of life. This was certainly the icing on the cake for me. I had thoroughly enjoyed my police service and worked with some wonderful, dedicated people, so accepted the honour on behalf of all my female colleagues. It was good to know that we had finally made our mark.

On Division, I became Bronze Commander for a number of the major events in the town. These included the rather prestigious annual River Festival, which used to attract up to a quarter of a million visitors over two days. The event had a number of attractions located on both sides of the River Ouse. These included a main stage with various bands, community events, a fun fair, a street parade, boat races, a raft race and a firework display. It was an enjoyable event to police, as most people were in festive mood and well behaved.

My biggest challenge came when we had a suspected improvised explosive device left under a bench. This was still a time of heightened security in mainland UK after several IRA bombings in the 1990s, so every suspect package was taken seriously.

I was on patrol at the site and made the decision to quietly evacuate people from a park area to the other side of the river without causing panic, while the bomb squad were called to attend, check and defuse the package. It was the first time I'd ever had to stop a fairground big wheel and empty the bumper cars, but fortunately, the fairground people worked well with the police and we cleared the site with a minimum of disruption. The suspect package turned out to be a rucksack containing a picnic and a transistor radio with the headphone wire trailing out of the bag. The bomb squad rearranged someone's sandwiches with a controlled explosion!

Fortunately, on hearing the bang, most festival-goers just seemed to think that they had missed an impromptu fireworks display and carried on enjoying the festival.

The Superintendent's role necessitated me being on rota call as public order Silver Commander for the County. Public order units predominately comprised of male officers. Although female officers could volunteer for the role, only a few did so.

I hadn't been back at Bedford for very long when the Chief Superintendent told me that there was trouble brewing in the Queen's Park area of Bedford, normally a very peaceful multi-cultural residential area. On this occasion, tension had built up between a group of young Muslims and a group of young Sikhs, There had already been a fight and petrol bombs thrown at a building, and now there were hundreds out on the streets supporting each side. Reports came in that the Sikhs were carrying knives and the Pakistanis were using hockey sticks as weapons and they were all making their way down to a green area near the river.

It's sometimes tempting to leave them to fight it out and pick up the pieces, but innocent people could get hurt so I deployed our Public Order Unit and attended as Silver Commander.

On arrival in Queens Park, the fully kitted Police Support Units (PSUs) waited in vans in the side streets, while I went with my tactical advisor (Inspector) to speak to the community leaders who were out on the streets. We strode through the volatile crowd and sought out the elders in the groups and called them together. It was obviously a surprise when they realised that it was a woman in charge, but they soon started to listen to orders to disperse when they realised that I had a strong, well-equipped team behind me. The community leaders had authority within their groups and after consultation they agreed to get the youngsters to disperse. The PSUs were deployed in a low-key manner, to help them on their way. Once the area was clear, I organised a meeting at Greyfriars Police Station to mediate and resolve issues.

I was always grateful to have an Inspector as tactical advisor and was not afraid to listen to his advice before making a decision, as this was a steep learning curve for me. On the other hand, when dealing with a potentially violent situation, it was very satisfying to be able to apply the training and win through as a unit. After the adrenalin flow, there was an immense feeling of relief that all had gone well.

When I returned to the police station, I went to see the Chief Superintendent, who unbeknown to me had been monitoring the action on CCTV. He said he was very happy with the way I'd dealt with the incident, but laughed saying that when I was in full flow I was quite frightening and reminded him of Boadicea going into battle! I was secretly quite flattered, but it was also a lesson to me to learn where all the CCTV cameras were in the town. Proliferation of CCTV cameras across Britain has fuelled speculation that the British are the most watched nation on the planet, but not only are the public being watched, as police action is also closely monitored.

My new post also required me to take on the role of Firearms Silver Commander.

I attended a course at the National Firearms Training Centre at Exeter, which would equip me to become part of a regular cadre of Superintendents on a County-wide rota. I was not an authorised firearms officer, as females had previously been barred from such training, so once again, I was on a steep learning curve. The training course covered both the theory and practical role of a Firearms Silver Commander and we were tested during practical exercises in the Exeter area. Having passed the test, I returned to Force, ready to take on the new responsibility.

Although I was used to shift work, being on call alternate weeks for public order or firearms was very tiring and could be stressful. My husband was at that time also a Superintendent in the Hertfordshire Constabulary and sometimes our on-call times coincided. On the dressing table in the bedroom we would have our landline phone, two mobile phones and two pagers, as well as a manual of firearms procedures.

I'm a light sleeper, so I tend to wake instantly when disturbed, whereas my husband sleeps deeply. I would, therefore, be first to respond to any of the calls, only waking him if necessary. One night, I thought I was dreaming when I heard movement and the clanking of a chain in the bedroom, but on investigation I found that I had left my pager on vibrate mode and it was running along the glass top of the dressing table dragging behind it the chain that I used to attach it to my belt!

I always had my uniform hanging up ready, so if I authorised the deployment of firearms, I could get dressed quickly and go to the scene. My husband would stir, just sufficiently to know that I was going out to a firearms job and then instantly drop off to sleep again. I was always a bit jealous of leaving him tucked up in the warm, but also a bit peeved that he didn't lie awake worrying about me!

In the UK, we still have a predominantly unarmed Police Service, but in order to be able to deal with criminals and terrorists who use firearms, every Police Force in the UK has a Firearms Unit. Police receive thousands of calls every year relating to suspected armed criminals and these calls may result in sending armed officers to investigate. They may subsequently have to discharge their firearms to protect themselves, the public or their colleagues and this may result in the death of a suspect.

As Silver Commander, my role was to assess evidence presented and decide if there was reason to believe that a suspect had a firearm that he was likely to discharge, causing danger to the public or to an officer. There are strict criteria and protocols to be observed before authorising the deployment of a firearms unit. The Silver Commander then attends the scene and sometimes a negotiator would be called. As the scenario develops all decisions and actions are recorded on a log and monitored by a member of the Force Executive, who becomes Gold Commander.

Fortunately, the firearms jobs that I commanded all went smoothly and suspects were disarmed without shots being fired, but I was very much aware that this wasn't always the case.

In 1998, my colleague, the Chief Superintendent, was on call and issued an authority for a firearms team. Bedford police subsequently shot dead Michael Fitzgerald, aged thirty-two, following an investigation into an alleged burglary. The deceased, who had returned home from the pub without his door key, had broken into his own home and subsequently been mistaken for a burglar. He was depressed, a heavy drinker and a John Wayne fan who had a collection of replica firearms, one of which he had been pointing directly at the Authorised Firearms Officer (AFO) who had to make a judgement call. Press headlines later read 'Police Shoot Unarmed Man in Own Home'.

The AFO and Chief Superintendent were both suspended from firearms duties pending an inquest and full investigation by the Independent Police Complaints Commission. In this case, the inquest returned a finding of lawful killing, but it was a stressful time for the officers involved, as potentially there can be allegations of criminal offences. It was against this background that we all carried out our duties. We knew that decisions made necessarily in haste, would be picked over at great length by experts and lawyers in their offices.

Before going off duty, it was the Superintendent's job to prepare an incident report for the Assistant Chief Constable's attention the following morning. During the day we had a secretary who was highly proficient and typed all my reports and letters, but at night I had to type my own. We had only recently been provided with desktop computers and I was still developing my computer skills. When I was tired it took me a long time to type out a full report in a presentable fashion, without margins and schedules jumping all over the place. I could have asked another officer to do it for me, but it was a matter of pride that I completed it myself and I found it quite exhausting. I very rarely slept properly when I got home to bed after a firearms or public order incident, especially if I knew that I had to be up for important meetings that same day.

After a year in the rank of Superintendent, I felt that I had proved that I could perform the role to a high standard. I was lucky to have survived thirty-four years in the police service physically and mentally intact, and without any blots on my personal record. I felt that I had overcome all the obstacles and reached the pinnacle of my career. I knew that there were now many career minded young men and women on the promotion ladder, so at the age of fifty three, it was highly unlikely that I would be considered for further promotion.

One night, when I was working late in the office after a call-out, I began to think about my future. My husband had already retired, I was eligible for a full pension and I wanted to finish my service on a high. As the year 2000 approached, it seemed eminently sensible to start the new millennium with a new lifestyle. I made the decision that night to retire in 2000 and submitted a report to this effect.

As I celebrated New Year's Eve 1999, I knew that I had made the right decision. The pace of change during my service had been relentless and continued to be so. I had been very proud to serve as a member of the British Police Service and genuinely believed that we did a good job. The police service would continue to attract keen, dedicated young men and women who would hopefully feel the same, but who would be operating a new policing model. I knew that, with increasing political and financial restrictions, I could not be happy with many of the necessary changes, so it was time for me to take up new challenges elsewhere.

After retirement, my husband and I moved to Devon. I love the countryside, the moors and the beautiful coastline, and feel that this is my 'spiritual home' where I can be truly happy. My hobbies include photography, painting landscapes, golf and being a guest speaker on cruise ships. My subject is 'Blue Line – Pink Thread' the story of how women have been woven into the fabric of the police service.

As I now reflect upon my police service, I realise how fortunate I was to have had a varied and fascinating career doing a job that I loved. I had joined the police service with the highest ideals of protecting the public and preventing crime and had always done my best to achieve this. Initially, I had no desire for promotion but my ambition had developed over the years, often because I felt that I could do the job as well as, if not better than, some of my male bosses. There weren't always suitable female role models so, on achieving promotion, I tended to roleplay the part, projecting myself in a way that I thought others expected. With training and experience, I gained in confidence and grew into the various roles. Eventually, I learned to be my own person, less worried about what other people thought about me and more committed to staying true to my own principles of honesty, fairness and service to the public.

In 2015, women police celebrate the centenary of the first British policewoman to be granted a power of arrest but there is now so much more to celebrate. The last thirty years have brought about many changes for women police officers as they have gained equality with their male colleagues and are now an integral and valued part of the 'Thin Blue Line'.

The first woman to hold the rank of Chief Constable was Pauline Clare who was appointed Chief Constable of Lancashire Constabulary in June 1995.

By 2013 there were six female chief constables, including Colette Paul as Chief Constable of Bedfordshire, and female officers were represented in all ranks and roles throughout the police service.

I have enjoyed the journey, witnessed many changes and sometimes pioneered them but it has not been without frustration and a few private tears. Above all, I feel immense pride to have worked as part of the police service and with a dedicated team of men and women. They continue to have my admiration and support.

Much to my surprise and delight, on 26th June 2015, I felt as though I had truly come full circle when I was invited to attend a ceremony at Bedfordshire Police Headquarters. This was to celebrate the retirement of Chief Constable Colette Paul, but she also had a surprise for me. To mark the 100th anniversary of women in policing, she honoured me by naming the headquarters lecture theatre as the 'Carole Phillips Theatre'. She cited the fact that back in 1974, I had been instrumental in getting female police officers to work on the front line, doing the same job as their male colleagues and earning equal pay.

I travelled up to Bedfordshire with my husband Martin and daughter Michelle and was proud to have them there as they have supported me throughout my career. I was delighted to accept the honour as recognition of the dedication and hard work of all those women who, over the years, tackled the many challenges of a career in policing. They have ensured that equality is here to stay and I think it's wonderful to have a name plaque while I'm still alive!

I hope that you have enjoyed reading these memoirs and that I have managed to convey a sense of the excitement, challenges, drama and sheer joy of being a policewoman.